Debt-Conversion Schemes in Africa

Debt-Conversion Schemes in Africa

LESSONS FROM THE EXPERIENCE
OF DEVELOPING COUNTRIES

AFRICAN CENTRE
FOR MONETARY STUDIES
and
ASSOCIATION OF
AFRICAN CENTRAL BANKS
in association with

JAMES CURREY
London

HEINEMANN
Portsmouth (N.H.)

African Centre for Monetary Studies *and*
Association des Banques Centrales Africaines
Association of African Central Banks
15 Boulevard Franklin Roosevelt
BP. 1791 Dakar

James Currey Ltd
54b Thornhill Square
Islington, London N1 1BE

Heinemann Educational Books Inc.
361 Hanover Street
New Hampshire 03801

92 93 94 95 96 5 4 3 2 1

British Library Cataloguing in Publication Data

African Centre for Monetary Studies
    Debt-Conversion Schemes in Africa:
    Lessons from the Experience of Developing Countries
    I. Title
    II. Association of African Central Banks
    332.4

ISBN 0-85255-138-X Cloth (James Currey)
ISBN 0-85255-137-1 Paper (James Currey)

ISBN 0-435-08080-6 Cloth (Heinemann)

Typeset by Colset in 10/13pt Times with Helvetica display
Printed in Great Britain by Villiers Publications, London N6

Contents

Preface

The purpose of this study is to provide, in a summary form, a review of the various types of market-based debt-reduction schemes, describing the main issues involved and assessing their applicability in African countries so as to assist the authorities of countries that may be contemplating the application of such schemes.

The study, therefore, attempts, for selected market-based debt-reduction schemes, to:

(i) describe and assess the patterns, structures and mechanisms used;

(ii) identify the benefits and drawbacks from the point of view both of the debtor country and of the creditors;
(iii) spell out the institutional pre-requisites for successful debt-reduction operation;
(iv) investigate the scope for their implementation in African countries; and
(v) analyse the cost-benefit calculus and the macroeconomic impact on the debtor country.

While the findings point to some scope both for debt-equity conversion and for debt buy-backs in some African countries, these mechanisms are not regarded as significant for either reducing the stock of debt or boosting investment in the majority of African countries. Even for those countries where full-fledged programmes for market-based debt-reduction schemes are endorsed, it is cautioned that they are likely by themselves to have only a limited impact on reducing the debt stock and should, therefore, be regarded as only one of a number of options that the African debtor countries should consider. In this regard, the report also recommends the pursuit of collective African bargaining for other international initiatives to open up further avenues in the area of debt conversion and debt buy-backs for the effective reduction of the region's external debt burden.

The study benefited from a Ford Foundation grant for which the Centre is deeply grateful. It also received technical assistance from the Commonwealth Fund for Technical Assistance. A draft of the study was discussed at a workshop organized by the Centre at UNCTAD in May 1991 and attended by Dr M.I. Mah'moud, Director of Research, ACMS (Chairman); Mr S.M. Malleck Amode, ACMS substantive economist for the study; Dr Y. Dembele, ACMS; Dr E.A. Ajayi and Mrs F.M. Yemidale, Central Bank of Nigeria; Mrs A. Trans-Nguyen, UNCTAD; Dr J.C. Berthelemy, OECD Development Centre; and Dr Matthew H. Martin, Oxford University and consultant to the study. The Centre wishes to express its appreciation of the valuable comments of these participants at the workshop.

A.K. MULLEI
Director General
African Centre for Monetary Studies
Dakar, Senegal

1

Types
of Market-Based
Debt-Reduction
Schemes

Introduction

Debt conversion in its various forms, in particular debt-equity
conversion but also buy-backs and other market-based debt-
reduction mechanisms, has in the most recent period come to be
regarded as a promising method of alleviating the commercial
component of the external debt burden of developing countries,
including its servicing. Latin American countries in particular,
but also some South-East Asian countries, have managed in certain cases to reduce their stock of commercial external debt

substantially, thereby easing foreign payments problems, by instituting formal debt-conversion programmes, sometimes with significant donor support, at other times totally by their own resources. At the same time, however, experience has revealed a certain number of problems that emerged as adverse side-effects of these programmes. Nonetheless, in face of the reluctance of the international economic community to convene a conference to address, in determined fashion, the debt problem of Africa as a whole, a relatively small number of African countries have begun implementing similar debt-conversion programmes, in order to capture some of the benefits of these transactions, including whatever prospects they offer for reducing the stock of debt and easing the debt-service burden. A few more of them engage sporadically in informal debt-conversion transactions, and are contemplating the possibility of instituting formal ones after analysing the mechanisms, the benefits and costs, and the other potential impacts on the macro economy.

Until the decision to undertake this study was taken, there was no well researched guide or blueprint for decision-makers on debt-equity conversions, or on other conversion mechanisms. When programmes were implemented in individual countries, the task of designing a programme and of setting up the institutional mechanism to implement it was often entrusted to an investment bank and/or an accountancy firm. True, *Euromoney* publications and the Economist Intelligence Unit had published surveys of debt-swap transactions as interest in the matter evolved, but not until the United Nations Centre on Transnational Corporations (UNCTC), in co-operation with the Latin American Economic System (SELA), issued, in March 1990, its report *Debt Equity Conversions: a Guide for Decision-Makers*, did a serious, usable document become available for decision-makers and practitioners to refer to.

The purpose of the present study is in one respect broader, but in all other respects far less ambitious, than the UNCTC report. It investigates the working not just of debt-equity conversion mechanisms but also of other market-based debt-reduction schemes that are likely to be of interest to indebted African countries as instruments to help ease their commercial external debt burden. The official-debt component of Africa's debt problem is analysed in a related but separate study on 'The Efficiency of Debt-relief Measures for African Countries'.[1] Although the commercial-debt component amounts to only about a third of the total debt stock of African countries, the incidence on the region's middle-income countries of servicing difficulties as regards this component of the debt is considerable, both as they affect inflows of resources for their development programmes and as they reduce imports, thereby shifting down both the output-growth and the consumption paths. The relatively recent emergence of a secondary market for Africa's external debt instruments and the growing importance of this market in the scope it offers to convert or retire the debt at the significant discounts that prevail, have fostered interest in market-based debt-reduction schemes as an efficient method of alleviating the debt burden. Numerous market-based schemes have been devised and utilized by different countries, among which the most popular fall into the categories of debt-equity swaps, debt buy-backs, debt securitization, and schemes based on a menu of these options. In addition, there are other minor schemes such as debt-for-exports, debt-for-nature and debt-for-development mechanisms, as well as other ad hoc conversion techniques which we do not investigate in this study because their impact on actually reducing Africa's debt burden is not likely to be significant.

A market-based debt-reduction scheme refers to a set of transactions made through the existing secondary market for a given debtor country's external debt, that are aimed at exchanging debt instruments into other forms of liabilities with a view to easing the debt stock and/or the debt-service burden, most often by capturing a large part of the discount on the secondary market. Such transactions involve the modification of the terms of the original debt contracts or their retirement in exchange for the issue of new liabilities such as equity instruments or other debt instruments of lower face-value, lower interest, longer maturity,

---

[1]ACMS: 'The Efficiency of Debt-relief Measures for African Countries', unpublished, ACMS, Dakar, 1991.

or any combination of these, or, indeed, in the case of buy-backs, in exchange for cash at lower than face-value. The gain by way of debt reduction, then, is exactly equal to the difference between the face-value of the debt and the present value of the new liabilities or the cash paid up. Importantly, it is possible that the currency denomination for interest servicing or for repayment of the debt will also be changed from foreign to local currency. All four broad types of market-based debt-reduction schemes listed above fit this general description, and the rest of this first chapter will describe each scheme in some detail, pointing out some of the features that explain each one's appeal.

Debt-equity swap

A debt-equity swap is a transaction that converts the debtor country's external debt into equity in a domestic firm. This new liability – the equity instrument – is generally acquired by a foreign investor, but this needs not to be so, especially when debt-equity transactions aiming to stimulate the repatriation of flight capital encourage or at least allow nationals to buy into domestic enterprises through the conversion schemes by using the capital they previously held abroad. A debt-equity swap involves the investor exchanging a country's debt (which often it has pre-viously acquired by buying it at a discount on the secondary market) at the Central Bank for local currency to be used in equity investments. Usually, these schemes carry some restrictions on remittance rights, on the types of investments allowed, and on the sale of the equity. The types of debt-equity swaps of relevance to African countries fall into three categories, only the first two of which have attracted sizeable deals. First, public sector debt can be exchanged for equity in a private sector enter-prise, either in the form of direct equity or portfolio investment. Secondly, public sector debt can be exchanged for equity in a para-public company that is being privatized as part of the debtor government's overall privatization programme. The major por-tion of such swaps are of the direct investment type rather than portfolio investment. Thirdly, the debt of a private company can be exchanged for equity investment in the same company. This third type is relatively rare for most African countries, because most long-term external debt is government-guaranteed. Debt-equity conversions require the prior insertion of special provisions in the loan agreements, and these are commonly included during rescheduling agreements. The already mentioned restrictions on the repatriation of remittances, besides providing relief and a breathing-space for the debtor, serve to prevent the new investors from obtaining more advantageous terms than the bank creditors. Furthermore, innovative variations have recently been made whereby closed-end conversion funds are created in which foreign debt is converted into risk capital and pooled to fund longer-term, large-size investment projects.

The relative – and growing – popularity of debt-equity swap programmes derives from the advantages that all sets of actors perceive them to offer as a way out of the quagmire of the continuing debt problem. There are three main actors in a debt-equity swap: the debtor/host country for investment, the investor, and the original creditor. In a typical situation, the original creditor, whether a bank or a trade-credit supplier holding a debt instrument of a given face-value, assesses the price of the instrument at a significant discount made manifest to one and all in the secondary-market price. At the given price, the original creditor considers it a fair deal to sell its debt or to convert it into an equivalent asset or indeed to hold on to it. On the other hand, the debtor is under obligation to service the debt under terms consistent with its face-value, even though it has difficulty in doing so. If it has a debt-equity conversion programme in place, it offers incentives for any holder of the debt to convert it into equity so that it happens that both the investor shares in the investment risk and the debtor reduces its debt stock. The investor can be the creditor bank itself or a secondary holder of the debt. Where the investor is the original creditor bank, it finds the swap appealing because it trades the near-certainty of a loss on its asset equivalent to the discount for the possibility of gain perhaps near to face-value or even above if the investment project is successful, tempered, of course, by the possibility of total loss. Where the investor is a secondary holder of the debt, he can gain both by cashing in on the discount on the secondary market and by offering himself the possibility of investment profits tempered by possible loss. In the latter case, the original creditor bank also finds a debt-equity swap appealing because it can obtain tax credit through the materialization of its loan loss. Finer details of the advantages and disadvantages of debt-equity swaps are discussed in Chapter 5.

Debt buy-back

The debt buy-back operation is the simple buy-back, for cash and at secondary-market prices, of its own debt by the debtor, in order to reduce its obligations at a discount. Normally, the financing for the buy-back comes from the country's foreign-exchange reserves, but there have also been a certain number of third-party-financed buy-backs where the resources come from outside grants given for this specific purpose. Strictly speaking, for a country to use its reserves openly for a buy-back operation, it requires the prior approval of all its creditors. This is secured during rescheduling operations. The prior-approval requirement is justified, first by the fear that the use of its reserves might impair the debtor's ability to service its remaining debt, and, secondly, by the moral hazard problem whereby the creditor stands to lose if the debtor is thereby encouraged to take actions to lower the price at which its debt is trading, in order to cash in the higher discount. This prior-approval requirement necessitates two amendments to the loan contracts. Firstly, the debtor must be allowed to prepay its loans. Secondly, participating creditors must be given waivers from sharing provisions, so that they do not have to share the payments they receive from the debtor country with non-participating creditors.

Because of these pre-conditions, buy-back operations have been significantly less frequent than debt-equity operations. Even so, as effective solutions to the overall debt problem become more and more elusive, and as the pressure for debt relief through outright write-off in the case of Africa intensifies, bank creditors are gradually becoming more receptive to requests from a couple or so of lower-middle-income African countries to buy back part of their debt, in the context of a package comprising other reconstitution measures including rescheduling and debt-equity conversion. The buy-back has two types of appeal to the creditor. The small creditor finds it a neat way of exiting from a problem area of operation at 'fair' cost. The transaction allows the small creditor to obliterate the need to make loan-loss provisions and cuts down staff time used to monitor the loan, adjust the accounts and so forth. He also obtains part payment on a loan which possibly could continue to depreciate in value. For the larger creditor, if the requirement for an open buy-back is fulfilled that all creditors agree to the buy-back exercise, reflecting their confidence that the debtor's ability to pay is not impaired, the appeal rests in reducing its exposure while maintaining the book-value of its remaining debt, if this is made at market prices. Furthermore, the creditor can obtain tax credit when the loan loss materializes. As for the debtor, the obvious gain is the secondary-market discount that it is able to capture. More detailed analysis of the costs and benefits of debt buy-backs is undertaken later in this study.

Besides the open buy-back, 'secret buy-back' operations are also possible and are reported to have actually been undertaken by several sovereign debtors. In the 'secret buy-back', instead of carrying out the transaction himself or openly through an agent after having secured the prior approval of all the creditors, the debtor short-circuits these and uses the services of an agent to buy back his debt anonymously. As mentioned above, this operation opens up the possibility for the debtor to take actions to depress the price artificially on the secondary market just prior to secretly buying back his debt. And the debtor does not deprive himself of this possibility, quite the contrary! By sending the appropriate 'signals', such as announcing particularly pessimistic foreign-exchange flow projections and budget deficits during the annual government budgetary exercise, the debtor country can cause the secondary-market price to fall, even temporarily, and this would be sufficient to allow it to cash in a higher discount. While such a strategy generally becomes known relatively soon after the transaction is successfully carried out and in theory can adversely affect future debt-reconstitution negotiations with creditors, it is also possible, in certain cases, to secure tacit acquiescence, because symmetrical strategies are followed by creditors as well. A well-researched literature has recently blossomed on the concept of market-signalling and reputation-building which sheds light on the theoretical subtleties of these strategies. The main point is that the initiating action to buy back the debt should assume complete rationality on the part of the creditor as well, and it should be recognized that any short-term windfall gain will have to be made good later and may increase uncertainty.

Debt-securitization

A debt-securitization operation is a transaction that involves the retiring of existing unsecuritized debt in exchange for new debt that is backed by collateral, either for interest payments or for principal repayment or for both. Because the new debt issued is collateralized, a significant portion of the old debt is reduced in the process, so that the existing debt is traded in for new debt not at par but at a significant discount, usually that prevailing on the secondary market. The new collateralized debt is excluded from future possible rescheduling, and it is more easily marketable precisely because it is securitized. The collateral offered to back interest payments, principal repayments, or both, can take the form of gilt-edge debt instruments from financial authorities of impeccable reputation such as the US Treasury, as was the case for the famous Morgan-Mexico debt securitization deal of 1988, or, conceivably, the World Bank, the International Monetary Fund or a new institution specifically set up for the purpose by both institutions, as has been proposed by Peter Kenen, Jeffrey Sachs and others in the suggestions for a new 'International Debt Facility'.[2] We consider in more detail the working of a concerted

[2] Jeffrey Sachs, *Efficient Debt Reduction*. International Economics Department WPS 194 World Bank Washington DC: 1989.

debt-reduction mechanism using the securitization procedure in Chapter 6 of this study where multilateral, concerted debt-reduction schemes in general are discussed.

A debt-securitization operation which offers collateral for the repayment of principal through gilt-edge zero-coupon bonds that the debtor may have purchased in itself offers real debt reduction only if the purchase price of the bonds relative to their face-value implies a fixed rate of interest significantly higher than the expected average rate likely to prevail on the (floating-rate) debt obligation during its period to maturity. This is tantamount to saying that, having borrowed at floating rates whose average expected level during the remainder of the period to maturity is relatively high, the debtor can obtain reduction of its debt only by purchasing gilt-edge bonds that yield even higher implicit fixed rates. Such a situation is possible if the purchase price of the bonds is a relatively small fraction of the face-value, as was the case in the US Treasury Bonds specially issued to back Mexico's debt-securitization programme. In addition, however, the terms under which the original debt instruments are traded for the new instruments can also offer reduction possibilities. Because the new debt is collateralized, it exchanges at a premium against the old debt, so that, for a given amount of original debt retired, a lesser amount of new collateralized debt is issued. Alternatively, if the two types of debt exchange at par, the rate of interest on the new debt is lower.

The debt-securitization deals that have so far been made have concentrated on collateralizing the principal repayments only, and this fact seems to have been a major obstacle to the mechanism's widespread adoption by the creditor community. It would be possible to collateralize both principal and interest payments, but then gilt-edge financial instruments other than zero-coupon bonds would need to be introduced and purchased. In that case it is not clear how the first source of gain by way of debt reduction described above would still be applicable; such a new instrument would sell at a competitive market rate, and the only debt-reduction gain to the debtor would arise from the second source, the capture of the discount on the secondary market. But this can be achieved by outright buy-back of the debt. Securitization through the issue of commodity bonds or through concerted debt-reduction mechanisms is also possible, and the latter are discussed more fully in Chapter 6.

The menu approach

Each of the above operations has feedback effects on the price in the secondary market, and creditors not participating in any one of the schemes may find the market value of the remaining debt affected by these operations. We have, in fact, pointed out above that the prior approval of all creditors is normally required before a conversion operation can proceed. As a result of these considerations, many creditors prefer a menu approach for debt reconstitution and debt reduction. The menu would include rescheduling, possibly with longer repayment periods and even interest caps, as well as part buy-back, part debt-equity swaps and part debt-securitization deals.

The interest-cap approach involves putting a ceiling on the interest payments of the debt and, if necessary, capitalizing the amount by which due interest payments exceed the ceiling and adding it to the principal for future amortization. This excess amount is, of course, variable because interest rates on all recent commercial loans have been floating. Furthermore, there may be no necessity to capitalize the interest due, because in restructuring negotiations it may be agreed that the creditors not participating in pure buy-backs implicitly offer a discount on their debt equivalent to the secondary-market price for participating creditors' debt instruments. In such instances, the lowering of the interest rate provides a mechanism for equal-sharing clauses.

Such menu-based schemes, in close parallel to the Brady Plan proposal, are investigated and discussed in more detail in Chapter 6.

Convergence of creditor and debtor interests

The appeal of each of the above-mentioned types of market-based reduction schemes lies to a great extent in the fact that they offer significant scope for the convergence of both debtor and creditor interests. The possibilities for such convergence derive from the fact that all debt-conversion transactions, including debt-reduction schemes, have several characteristics in common with a bargaining game. While the terms of the original loan contract depict a situation where the gain of the debtor would be matched by a loss for the creditor through reduction in the market value – and eventually the realization value – of the debt instrument, the practical ability-to-pay considerations and the complex interplay of expectations make it possible for the interests of creditors and debtors to converge. In the first place, the severe impairment of the debtor's ability to pay leaves the creditor with the possibility, in the worst-case scenario, of the obligations he holds being simply repudiated, so that his asset has virtually no value. On the other side is the debtor, who unarguably has an obligation to repay a loan at its full face-value, and who could severely damage his access to further financing if he chooses the repudiation option. Yet the impairment of his ability to pay is very real, and at the same time the possibility of future improvement in his creditworthiness is not to be totally ignored. The scope for the convergence of creditor and debtor interests lies in striking a bargain to write down the debt partially so that, on the one hand, the creditor improves his repayment prospects from a near-zero-value worst-case scenario, and, on the other hand, the debtor effectively reduces his debt stock and thereby his debt-service burden, without resorting to the credit-worthiness-damaging repudiation option.

The theoretical literature investigating the more common case of an impairment of the ability to pay as opposed to the extremes of repudiation versus full servicing, points out that the best scope for a convergence of creditor and debtor interests arises when there exists a 'debt overhang'. This concept characterizes the conditions under which the debt burden has disincentive effects on the macroeconomic performance of the debtor country. One of the conditions is satisfied when the present value of the current and expected future ability to pay of the debtor is lower than the face-value of the debt contracted. In such a situation, the only amounts which the creditor receives in repayment are determined by the debtor's ability to pay. Furthermore, debt-servicing then acts like a distortionary tax on the economy, with a corresponding 'deadweight loss', since whatever proportion of additional growth in the debtor's economy goes towards debt-servicing is equivalent to a tax at a marginal rate equal to the proportion paid out. Thus, by reducing the debt to a level where it is in line with the debtor country's ability to pay, the debt becomes a lump-sum charge deductible from the additional growth instead of a marginal tax. The distinction is the same as that between a pool tax and a marginal tax: the latter is distortionary. As a consequence, debt reduction removes the disincentive to growth and is of more benefit to the debtor country. However, in so far as growth is not discouraged, it also benefits the creditor, because ability to pay subsequently improves. Some researchers however, have voiced empirically-based reservations about the idea of a debt overhang adversely affecting growth through the channel of lowered investment, and have proposed instead the alternative but related concept of a debt Laffer curve. According to this analysis, there is a debt overhang when the debt-repayment potential of the debtor country is a function of its debt stock. The function takes the form more or less of an inverted parabola, depicting the situation where the reimbursement potential increases as the stock of debt increases up to a certain point where the potential reaches a maximum, and thereafter decreases as the stock of debt continues to increase. This concept is in isomorphic correspondence with the Laffer curve in connection with tax revenues and increases in tax rates, hence the term 'debt Laffer curve' or 'Laffer curve for debt relief'. The idea is that, when the stock of debt is relatively small, lying below the amount at which the curve reaches its maximum, according debt relief only reduces the value of repayments, because at such levels the debt can be expected to be repaid integrally. Beyond the critical point, however, *refusing* debt relief causes the absolute value of repayments to decline because the disincentive efforts predominate.

Then the conditions for a debt overhang are satisfied, and granting debt relief is advantageous to the creditor, as well as benefiting the debtor.

A more detailed discussion, according to each type of debt-reduction mechanism, of the convergence of debtor and of creditor interests is presented in Chapter 5.

Overview of the study

Having defined the market-based debt-reduction mechanisms with which we shall concern ourselves in this study and having delineated the rationale for effort to be spent in implementing such schemes to the benefit of both debtors and creditors, we proceed in the following chapters to study the actual mechanisms of debt-conversion schemes using the secondary market, and to spell out the institutional pre-requisites that the implementing agency needs to put in place to carry out a major debt-reduction operation successfully. This important analysis, which can serve as a guide to debt managers who may consider implementing debt-reduction programmes using the elements identified above, is carried out in Chapter 2. It complements Chapter 3 which deals with the practice of debt conversion in important implementing countries, including African countries. Chapter 4 investigates the scope for debt-equity conversion and debt buy-backs in African countries. It characterizes the demand side by analysing the nature of financial paper offered on the secondary market for debt instruments, and in parallel investigates the supply side in terms of the nature of counterpart assets to be ceded. It concludes that there is significant scope both for debt-equity conversion and for debt buy-backs as mechanisms to reduce the external debt of at least some seven relatively diversified African countries, with non-negligible scope in an additional six. Chapter 5 analyses the cost-benefit calculus and the macroeconomic impact of debt conversion, again limiting the analysis to debt-equity swaps and debt buy-backs, leaving securitization and menu-based concerted debt reduction to Chapter 6. It brings out that, while there are considerable benefits deriving from these two types of debt-reduction mechanisms, there are also major drawbacks. The nature of these drawbacks is analysed and the experience of implementing countries in dealing with them studied. Possible solutions are also proposed. Finally, Chapter 6 looks at other methods of market-based debt-reduction schemes, focusing on concerted operations involving the multilateral financial institutions. Because the two other methods of market-based debt-reduction mechanisms – securitization and the menu approach – are best tackled, at least in the African case, in the context of concerted action, we have reserved detailed discussion of these two mechanisms for Chapter 6. A set of recommendations concludes the study.

2

The Mechanics of Debt Conversion

Overview of procedures

All debt-conversion transactions involve the surrendering of the initial, foreign-currency-denominated debt-note – either by the original lender or by a holder who had already bought it on the secondary market – for other assets of lower value issued by the original debtor or some other agent on his behalf. Since the original debt-note is denominated in foreign currency, the Central Bank of the debtor inevitably comes into play, as indeed it came into play when the debt was originally contracted. In

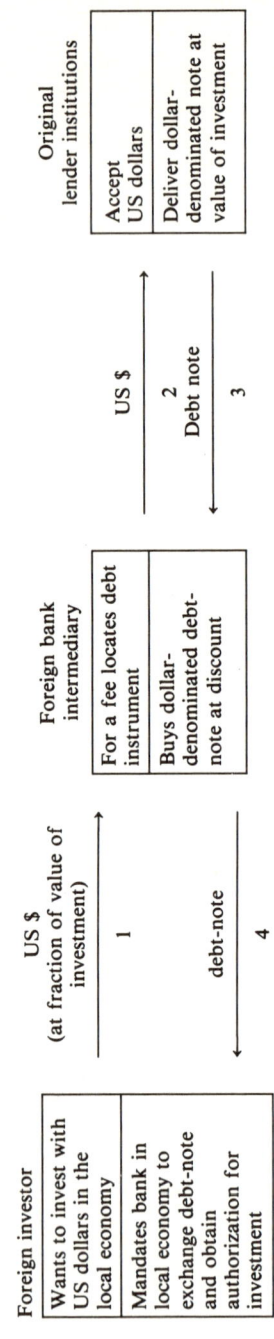

Fig. II.1   *Foreign sector component*

2. Domestic sector component

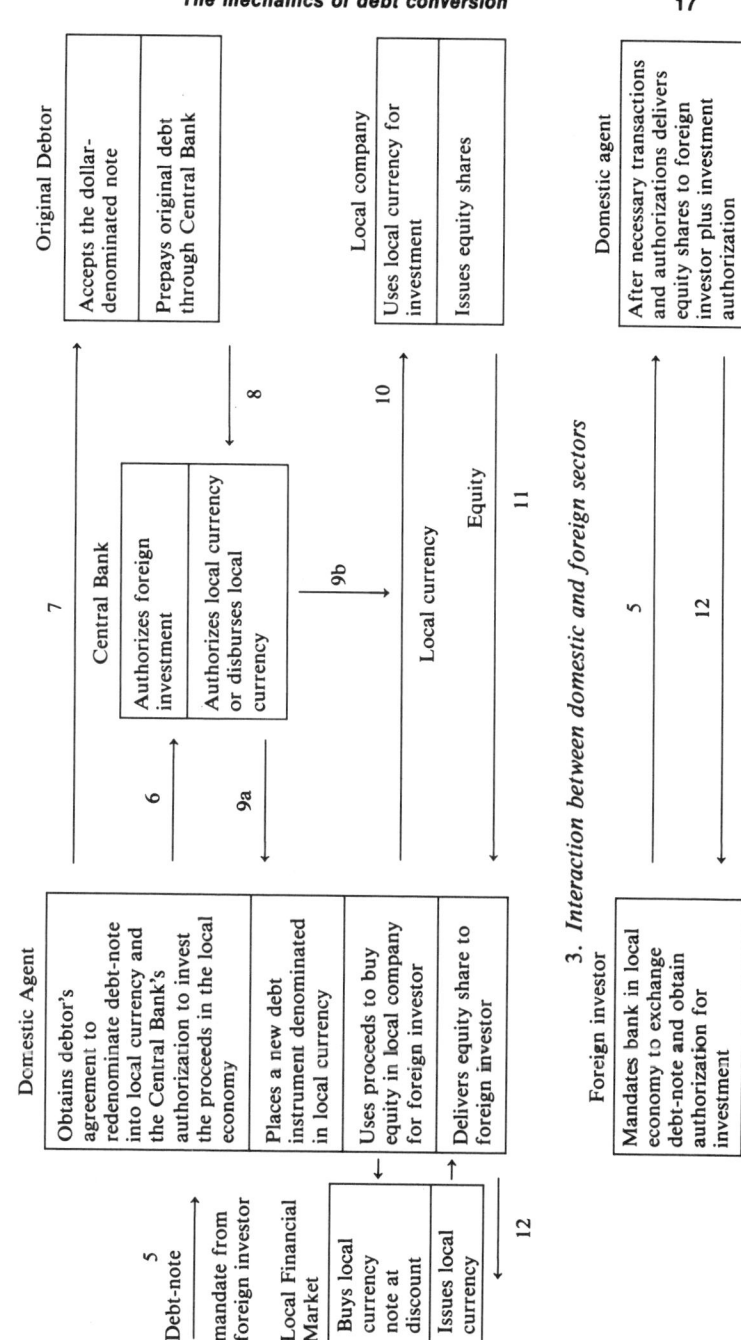

3. Interaction between domestic and foreign sectors

Source: Adapted from UNCTC/SELA Guide, which in turn was based on World Bank, *World Development Report 1987*. Washington, DC.

addition, for all cases of interest to us here, the individual debt-conversion programmes are devised by the Ministry of Finance or of the Economy, and are administered directly by the Ministry or through the Central Bank. Often there are intermediaries, or debt-rakers, that are also important players, and in certain schemes the multilateral financial institutions have a role to play. We shall examine in detail in the following section the parts played by the main actors in the various types of debt-conversion programmes, and analyse the forces and motivations at work. It is more illuminating however, to start with the procedures involved in a typical debt-conversion transaction, and for this purpose we investigate the working of the most complex type, the debt-equity swap.

Figure II.1 gives a diagrammatic presentation of the procedures involved in a typical debt-equity transaction. The two most important protagonists in a debt-conversion operation are the lender and the debtor, but the individual debt-equity swap transaction starts with a third party, a potential foreign investor, wanting to invest in foreign currency in a developing country that happens to have external debt which it wants to clear partially through a debt-swap programme. The potential investor is faced with two possibilities. Either to make a straightforward, traditional investment, in which case he pays foreign currency for the equity and other costs of setting up business in the host country at the official exchange rate. Or, more attractively if the host country has a debt-conversion programme and/or the country's debt can be bought on the secondary market and redeemed in local currency under specific terms, to purchase debt on the secondary market at a discount and redeem it with the debtor (and the debtor's authorities) in local currency for local investment in eligible projects. In this second case, the investor makes a front-ended profit on his investment because he capitalizes on the discount on the debt in the secondary market. The return-on-investment calculations of the potential investor are enhanced by this factor, and he may decide to go ahead with the project because of the mere fact of this added advantage, whereas he might otherwise have hesitated, withdrawn, or delayed the project. Both the investor and the debtor can gain from the scheme, and even the original creditor, where he is not the investor but a creditor bank that had sold part of its debt on the secondary market, could conceivably stand to gain. But more of this later. The actual implementation of even one formal debt-equity transaction is much more complex than the preceding simple description. Usually, the debt that a debtor country would want to make eligible for debt-equity conversion is held by the original lenders who happen to be commercial or merchant banks and who are in no significant way potential investors. So, the debt instruments that would normally be used by a potential investor in a debt-equity transaction comprise that marginal portion of the total commercial debt of the debtor country which the smaller banks have unloaded onto the secondary market while they were in search for an exit in order to avoid providing new money in conventional rescheduling exercises. (We shall take a look in the following section, at the extent – and, indeed, the thinness – of the secondary market for developing country debt). In consequence, the foreign investor, being a neophyte in this business, has to approach a foreign bank intermediary to source the eligible debt for him, and this is done for a fee. The foreign investor then has to contract the services of a domestic agent who, again for a fee, will handle for him all transactions involving securing agreement to redenominate the debt-note in local currency, the authorization of the Central Bank for the investment, the administration of the local currency proceeds as they are disbursed, and the procurement of the equity shares. Important parts are also played by the original debtor, the Central Bank (which may also charge a fee) and, most importantly, the local company in which the foreign investor acquires equity.

Much of the complexity and the fee structure involved in a debt equity deal depend on the individual case. These become even more difficult to characterize for the larger category of debt-conversion deals in general, because the number of both actors and transactions varies. Figures II.2 and II.3 give a diagrammatic representation of the procedures involved in a debt-conversion and in a debt buy-back transaction, respectively. The debt-for-local-currency swap is more complex than both of these, but less complex than the debt-equity swap, and its structure can be

Fig. II.2 *Diagrammatic presentation of the procedures for a debt-debt conversion transaction*

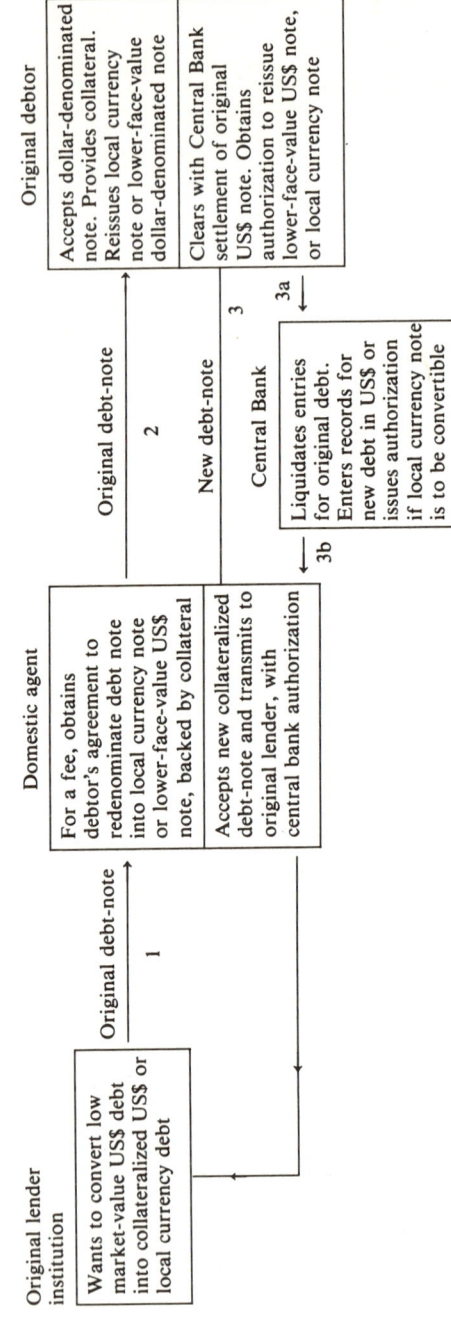

Source: Adapted from UNCTC/ECLAC Guide
Note: In many cases the intermediary bank can be by-passed and attendant costs saved.

Fig. II.3 *Diagrammatic presentation of the procedures for a debt buy-back operation*

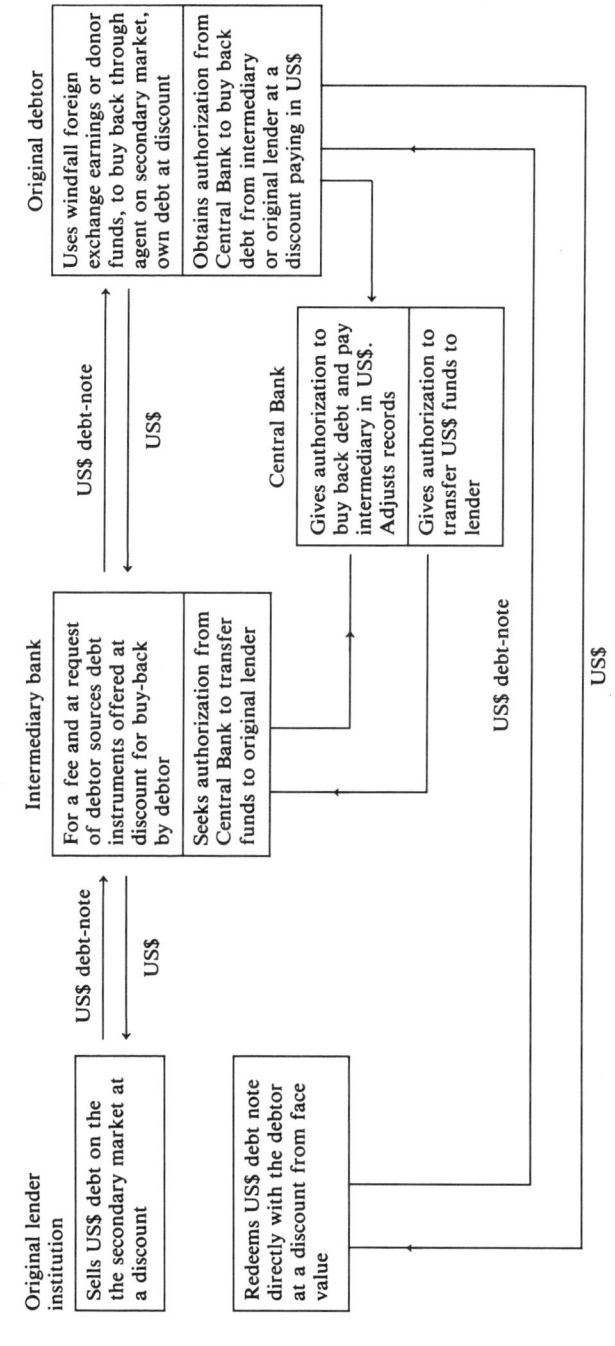

Source: Author's own design
Note: In many cases the intermediary bank can be by-passed and attendant costs saved.

deduced from a careful study of Table II.1. The debt-in-kind swap has an additional physical-goods dimension that makes it about as complex as the debt-equity swap. Regarding the fee structure, an idea of the dimensions may be grasped from the following hypothetical example, based on a composite of the near-middle-income African countries' debt, and inspired by an example given by the authors of the UNCTC/SELA *Guide for Decision Makers*.[1]

- Corporation A asks Bank B to assemble a package of $30 m. face-value of eligible debt of Country C, which it intends to use to finance an investment in that country through its debt-equity conversion programme. Bank B agrees to do this for $180,000.[2]

- Bank B then assembles the debt at an average price of 30 cents, which means Corporation A pays 2 per cent of $9 m., which is the market value of the $30 m. face-value debt. (Alternatively, Bank B may provide Corporation A with an option to buy this debt on the terms mentioned above, in which case an option fee of a further 1–2 per cent might be involved. The Bank then assumes the risk of holding the debt if the corporation subsequently declines to buy.)

- Corporation A, represented by Bank B, will then bid (through Broker D), either at the regular auction in Country C or in negotiations with the Central Bank and other Country C authorities, for the right to convert the debt it has bought, or on which it has an option, under the terms of the official debt-equity conversion programme or under agreed ad hoc terms. Based on a typical auction for one of the larger African countries in late 1990, it will probably have to bid at around a 48 per cent discount, and in the case of priority projects, the rate may be about 14.7 units of local currency to the dollar

---

[1] Antoine Basile, Andrew Hilton et al. *Debt Equity Conversions: A Guide for Decision Makers*. Report of the UNCTC/SELA, March 1990. UNCTC, New York. Draft Report, pp. 28–9.
[2] Ibid. Normally a flat fee, of the order of 2 per cent of the market value of the debt. The fee is flat rather than a percentage, to induce the Bank to get as low a price as possible for the debt.

compared to an official rate of 8 units to the dollar. This means that Corporation A redeems its purchased debt-note at $15.6 m. (still higher than the $9 m. actually paid), but in addition obtains a subsidized exchange rate, so that in effect it obtains nearly $28.7 m. worth of local currency at the official rate.[3] However, the Corporation may then have to pay a transaction commission to the Central Bank, which may be a percentage of the proceeds or a flat fee that may be equivalent to as high as 5 per cent of the proceeds. Corporation A would thus receive a net amount equivalent to about $27.25 m. or about $14.8 m., depending upon whether it qualifies for the exchange-rate subsidy or not. Finally, the Corporation may have to pay a fee to its agent bank which will be in the order of 0.5 per cent of the funds received – that is, $137,000 or $74,000 depending on the exchange-rate subsidy case, plus a fee of up to 2.5 per cent to the local broker ($681,000 or $370,000), all of these in local currency.

All in all, therefore, Corporation A will have its initial cost of $9 m. increased by various fees totalling about $2.4 m. or $1.4 m., depending on whether it benefits from an exchange-rate subsidy or not. However, it will still have received back $28.7 m. or $15.6 m. equivalent in local currency to invest in its project. This amounts to a very attractive deal if the only alternative for Corporation A to make its investment was to bring in new funds at the official exchange rate.[4]

Mirroring the complexity of the procedures on the investor's side, the host country's tasks in managing a debt-equity conver-

---

[3]It is to be noted that not all debt-equity conversions benefit from subsidized exchange rates and that the rate of the subsidy may differ from project to project.
[4]It must be pointed out that, strictly speaking, it is by no means necessary to use an intermediary bank or local brokers to do the transactions. Indeed, one of the most important countries to implement debt-equity transactions, Mexico, insists that swap' transactions can be arranged directly, without the use of intermediaries. Small investors are especially encouraged by Finance Ministry officials to avail themselves of the Ministry's consultative and administrative services. *The Economist Intelligence Unit* publication *Guide to Debt Equity Swaps*, Report No. 1104 of September 1987 reports that in a recent transaction a small foreign company saved itself $25,000 bank intermediary fees by completing the paperwork in one afternoon.

sion are equally involved and entail commensurately important costs as well as yielding handsome benefits. A full treatment of these benefits and costs is given in Chapter 5, but it is also important to look at the procedures that the debtor country has to set up to ensure a successful debt-equity conversion programme. A complete enumeration and discussion of all the procedures is not possible, although an *a priori* listing of the issues of importance is given in Chapter 5. Here we preview four crucial procedural factors to be considered: the selection of eligible investment projects and their priority ranking; the agreed disbursements schedule for the proceeds of the conversion; the administrative restrictions to be imposed on dividend payments and capital repatriation; and the exchange-rate subsidization mechanism or other incentive system.

Many countries already have a National Foreign Investment Commission, or its equivalent, whose function is to oversee the implementation of government priorities in investment in order to exploit in optimal fashion the domestic economy's natural and other resources, and to monitor the degree of foreign penetration and control of the domestic economy. In the context of the implementation of a debt-equity conversion programme, the NFIC has both a prior and a follow-up role to play. Its prior role is to establish the priority order of eligible investment projects and to set limits to the extent of foreign ownership; its regulations must be included in the debt-conversion guidelines. Its follow-up role is to monitor implementation of its directives and to revise priorities in the light of experience.

The second important procedural factor on the host-country side is to establish regulations to ensure that the proceeds of debt conversion are effectively used for the purposes approved and not diverted to alternative uses. Typically, host countries prohibit the use of debt-conversion funds to pay foreign banks, foreign suppliers or the foreign parent companies of domestic subsidiaries. The money also cannot be used for working capital, unless the capital is deemed to be essential to the development of an approved investment project and is not used for any payments abroad. The local-currency proceeds of the debt conversion are to be used only to pay the company's local suppliers, contractors and/or creditors, with proof of goods or assets exchanged. To ensure compliance, regulations almost invariably require that the funds go into a blocked account at the Central Bank or with a commercial bank under supervision of the Central Bank and the Ministry of Finance. At the time of the conversion, therefore, a disbursements schedule has to be agreed to allow funds to be released directly to the company's suppliers, contractors and/or creditors as bills become due and upon presentation of the necessary documents to be lodged with the Central Bank. Here, countries newly envisaging establishing debt-conversion programmes have to make an important decision as to whether interest can be earned by these blocked deposits until payments become due, and what should be the applicable rate. The most obvious choice, if interest is, indeed, to be paid, is the 90-day Treasury Bills rate, since the blocked deposits are only short-term. In view of complaints by investors through debt-equity conversion that inflation and exchange-rate movements make the blocked deposit idea a prohibitive factor, several countries have agreed to conversion in tranches to meet the local-currency requirements of a project financed by debt conversion as a whole from the very beginning.

Next, it is obviously necessary to have restrictions on the repatriation of capital, because otherwise the debt conversion becomes a drain on the implementing country's resources rather than a solution to its debt problem. Again, the choice that suggests itself is that investment capital should not be liquidated or transferred to a local investor before the date of maturity of the cancelled credit, and, perforce, capital should not be repatriated before the same date. However, it may be possible that the period to maturity of the debt instrument offered for conversion is of relatively short duration, say two years. A few countries have therefore specified the period before any repatriation of capital can be effected as between ten and twelve years or the maturity of the cancelled debt, whichever is the longer. In addition, there may be a need to restrict dividend payments as well for a certain period. In general, implementing countries are currently restricting dividends payments until three to five years after the initial investment is made. This proviso is analogous to the grace period granted during debt rescheduling operations, and serves the same purpose of allowing a breathing space.

Some of the merchant and investment bankers interviewed in the context of this study expressed the view that the scope for debt-equity conversion both to reduce the debt and to act as a foreign-investment catalyser in African countries would be greatly enhanced if there were functioning capital markets in the host countries. The interviewees spelled out that the existence of functioning capital markets would facilitate the raising of additional domestic capital and would also allow selling off shares in the investment project subsequently. In view of the capital remittance restrictions, however, which the interviewees accept as inevitable, their opinion can only be interpreted to mean that if there were sound indications today that, within the medium term of about five years, functioning capital markets would be operating in the host countries, that fact would enhance the scope for debt conversion. The next section of this chapter looks at the actual scope for debt conversion in selected African countries, in the context of these prior requirements, including the existence of a capital market.

Finally, the debt-conversion committee is also required to address the matter of setting the exchange-rate subsidization rate, or other incentive mechanism. This is done in tandem with the priority ranking established by the NFIC. Typically, the Central Bank, in consultation with the Ministry of Finance, sets the types of incentives that it is willing to provide in conversion arrangements to follow the priorities. In cases where an auction system is used to determine the discount at which the debt instrument is traded in, the incentive might take the form of a variable rate of subsidy on the exchange rate, with a higher subsidy going to a higher priority project. In cases where the discount is set administratively, the rate of discount may be made to vary with the order of priority, with a lower discount going to the higher priority project. Clearly any combination of the above measures, plus others besides, can be devised to vary the degree of incentive to investors in the projects preferred by the government.

The role of the secondary market

The term 'secondary market' for developing countries' external debt refers to that cluster of unregulated transactions in which the debt instruments of countries with certain economic problems, held by commercial banks but also partly by suppliers and owed usually by public entities but also by the private sector, are traded at a substantial discount in attempts by transactors to adjust their portfolios. The market is unregulated in that there is no central exchange through which prices are quoted publicly; it is highly imperfect and there is no obligation on anyone to deal at whatever offer or bid prices are made by individual transactors. The market is also very 'thin': of a total of bank and trade-related non-bank external claims estimated in mid-1990 at USS\$761 billion,[5] the total debt swap volume (including 'chain' transactions to acquire enough debt of a certain type for a debt deal as well as trade for purely speculation purposes) amounted to an upper limit of some \$20 bn a year.[6] Nonetheless, this market is not negligible, one of the reasons being precisely that the great popularity of debt-equity conversion transactions has given it vigour, translated into a high growth rate of volume traded in the last couple of years. More than 50 commercial and investment bank intermediaries are now reported in creditor countries with departments designated to deal in debt swaps, with the top eight accounting for more than 85 per cent of the volume.

As far as African debt is concerned, it has been estimated that, at the end of 1990, this market was trading in the debt of fifteen African countries. When interviewed, the staff of a major bank intermediary dealing importantly in debt swaps estimated that at least 50 per cent of the activity on the secondary market ends up in local projects via deals involving *bona fide* investors. On the

---

[5]This figure is from OECD/BIS semi-annual *Statistics on External Indebtedness*, January 1991.
[6]This upper-limit estimate is from the UNCTC/SELA Guide, op. cit. p. 19, but a Centre for Economic Policy Research (CEPR) discussion paper gives a figure of \$70 bn for 1989. See D. Cohen and R. Portes, *The Price of LDC Debt*, Discussion Paper No 459 of the Centre for Economic Policy Research, London, September 1990.

other hand, about 50 per cent of activity constitutes positions acquired by speculators for yield purposes. The overall size of the African market was estimated by traders in early 1991 to have totalled no more than $500 m. cumulatively for the period 1980–86. During the subsequent period 1986–9, the volume traded rose to an estimated $800 m. of final transactions (total transactions including double counting in 'chain' transactions, with instruments changing hands three or four times, exceed $1.8 bn.).[7] Even then trading focused on a few countries, with each country 'market' being quite tiny, with no more than one or two transactions a year. Information supplied by a leading trader on its estimate of the volume and frequency of transactions for a sample of the larger and more important African countries is as follows:

Nigeria: Nigerian debt traded on the secondary market is the largest, volume-wise, for any single African country. The volume traded varies significantly from week to week, but is estimated at more than $100 m.

Morocco: Between $50 m. and $75 m. per week, as a conservative figure.

Algeria: Slightly larger than Morocco.

Zimbabwe: (blocked dividend paper only) $25 m. per week.

Egypt: The market is particularly active for informal conversion by the government through a fronting institution. These operations are particularly successful. The government buys whenever the Egyptian Pound is favourable.
             The loans are non-performing, yet they are priced at 40 cents on the dollar.

Analysis of price formation in this secondary market for developing countries' external debt has failed to uncover any overriding determinants. A 1990 discussion paper by Daniel

---

[7]These figures, and a certain amount of the material in this chapter and parts of subsequent chapters, came from the informative book by Matthew Martin: *The Crumbling Facade of Africa's Debt Negotiations: No Winners* (London: Macmillan, March 1991). Dr Martin was a part-time consultant on this study.

Cohen and Richard Portes of the Centre for Economic Policy Research in London[8] used principal components analysis on data for the debt price of seven major debtor countries to isolate the most important variables and then proceeded to run normal long-linear relations between the variable and the secondary-market price of the debt to test their significance econometrically. The results of their investigation unveiled only one unmistakable determinant, the rate of interest, LIBOR, as the one identifiable variable influencing the price of debt, both short-term and long-term. Tests confirmed the *a priori* assumption that, as LIBOR increases, the price of debt comes down, in support of the argument that the price of debt is the discounted value of reduced future payments on account of debt servicing. Furthermore, the LIBOR elasticity of price was unity. This implied that debtors service their debt independently of its face-value, but contingent on other economic considerations, in particular the availability of 'spare' foreign exchange. On the other hand, there were indications that the price of long-term debt was scaled on the country's resources (i.e., the more significant the resources, the higher the price), and furthermore, that the price of long-term debt relative to *short-term debt* was influenced by the price of the debtor country's exports. In other words, when there was no breakdown of debt prices as between long-term and short-term instruments, the price of exports had no influence on the debt price. Nor did that variable have an influence when the price of long-term debt was taken in isolation. However, when the *relative* price of long-term vis-à-vis short-term debt was regressed on the price of exports, the estimate of elasticity was superior or equal to one. This points to the interpretation that the price of a country's exports matters for the service of the debt (at least, as debt traders on the secondary market perceive it), but this is only conditional on the decision to service short-term debt as a priority. The result makes good economic sense, since as a rule trade credits are defaulted on only as a last resort.

In addition to LIBOR, the other variables identified by the principal components analysis as having an effect on the price of

[8]Cohen and Portes, *The Price of LDC Debt*, op. cit.

short-term debt are lumped together by the authors as 'non-economic, idiosyncratic factors', such as political risk. Vague as this description is, it is shared by several other researchers in the field, who, in addition, include a country's payment record in the list of important variables. Furthermore, the important fact has been pointed out that the entire price curve for developing-country debt has itself been shifted periodically by exogenous factors independent of the debtor country's behaviour. The prime such factor often cited is the May 1987 announcement of Citicorp's decision to increase its provisioning on developing-country loan-loss reserves by $3 bn, or 25 per cent of its total exposure. It is worth noting, in this context, that a section of the financial press specializing in African news reported in early 1990 that the total provisioning of four important banks against Third World debt had exceeded the 50 per cent level. Standard Bank's provisioning level stood then at 58 per cent, Midland Bank's at 50 per cent, and Lloyds and National Westminster's both at 70 per cent. Some US banks were reported to be making 100 per cent provisioning. These factors would clearly have been causing frequent shifts in the entire price curve for developing countries' debt, and the situation explains the difficulty for econometric investigation to track down statistically significant determinants of price.

At an a *priori* theoretical level, a rigorous model can be built of the effect of various debt-trading and debt-conversion transactions on price *movements*, if assumptions of complete information, instantaneous adjustment and perfect competition are made for all participants, even if the number of participants is such as to imply oligopolistic behaviour. A more or less complete description of one such model is given in the Appendix. This model, though purely theoretical, will be important when we discuss institutional approaches to resolving the debt problem by using the market mechanism. For now, two important practical problems with the model need to be pointed out. Firstly, even if it explains price *movements* rigorously, the model assumes a starting discount from which the price movements take place. The question remains as to what determines the initial price level. The second problem is, of course, the objection commonly raised against rigorous theoretical models: that their assumptions are not borne out in fact.

The most vivid factual example offered to throw the empirical hollowness of the rigorous model into relief and to highlight the difficulties of identifying the main determinants of price on the secondary debt market was given by a leading debt trader during the 1988 *International Herald Tribune* Conference on Latin American Debt.[9] At a time when Brazilian debt was mostly being quoted at 42 cents on the dollar by banks which purportedly were following the market closely, four banks were approached to arrange a debt exchange of $200 m. for a large multinational company. This required the purchase of as much as $200 m. face-value of Brazilian paper. Since the company wanted to set the price, all four banks began sniffing out the market. On the strength of these factors alone (since there was no other demand for Brazilian paper), the price of Brazil's debt went up to 55 cents. In other words, the mere rumour of a possible purchase of no more than three-tenths of 1 per cent of the stock of Brazilian debt caused the price to jump by 30 per cent!

Besides highlighting the extreme volatility of price on the secondary market for debt, this example brings out the distinction that needs to be made between the bid price and the offer price. In the example, the offer price (the price the seller wants) averaged 42 cents initially, and presumably the bid price (the price the buyer will pay) which the multinational company wanted to set by asking four banks to feel the market, was intended to be lower. Instead, because this is an oligopoly situation with an amorphous mechanism, the rumour of a transaction caused the offer price to increase dramatically, leaving the buyer perplexed as to the bid price he could make.

In spite of the apparent irrationality in the above example, there are a certain number of constants, trends and determinant factors that are discernible, in addition to those spelled out above regarding LIBOR, payment record, and political risk. One constant is that prices are generally sticky upwards and fairly elastic

[9]The trader was Richard Marin of Bankers Trust. The whole episode is recounted in the UNCTC/SELA, *Guide for Decision Makers*, op. cit. p. 19.

downwards. It can also be said with a fair degree of confidence that the major economic indicators such as exchange-rate movements, budget deficits, inflation or GDP growth have almost no influence on price. We have seen above that changes in export commodity prices do have an influence on the price of long-term debt because of the impact they have on capacity to pay. For the debt of the larger countries, both long-term and short-term, factors such as successful reschedulings and IMF programme signings have a positive influence. Public breakdowns of IMF programme negotiations may have sudden large negative effects, while delays in rescheduling or the accumulation of payments arrears on new trade finance have gradual negative effects. Finally, the announcement of a debt-reduction plan often has an upward influence on prices. It is argued that this rise in prices occurs, not because it enhances the perceived creditworthiness of the debtor country, but because creditors push the offer price up in order to get a higher price in the reduction plan. Much the same hold-back-and-watch game on the part of banks has vitiated plans to set up a partially donor-backed facility to buy back developing-country debt at market discounts and pass on the gains to the debtor countries. We shall return to this later.

Analysis of the determinants of secondary-market price is important for countries envisaging debt-reduction programmes, since, in the case of buy-backs, the price determines the outlay required to effect any given reduction in the debt, while in debt-equity or other conversion programmes the secondary market price offers a yardstick against which negotiated prices and other terms may be assessed. Table II.1 gives the actual prices prevailing on four recent dates for the debt instruments of 19 African countries that were publicly quoted.

Before concluding this section, it may be instructive to give a brief description of the main actors on the secondary debt market and an approximate appraisal of the fee structure for intermediaries operating on the market. There are five categories of players: the host-country authorities for debt-equity conversion or (which is the same thing) the debtor country for other forms of debt reduction; the creditor banks or other creditors; the debt brokers; the foreign investors in the case of debt-equity

Table II.1 Secondary-market price spread of external debt instruments of selected African countries (US cents on $)

Country	29/11/90	19/12/90	27/12/90	17/01/91	Comment
Algeria	76-88	76-84	76-84	76-84	Price depends on maturity
Angola	35-40	35-40	35-40	35-40	Very quiet
Cameroon	37-40	37-40	37-40	37-40	Occasional deals
Congo	7-9	7-9	7-9	7-9	Lots of paper chasing a home
Côte d'Ivoire	2-5	2.5-5	3.25-4.25	3.25-4.25	Activity picks up again
Egypt	43-43.5	43-43.5	45-46	45-46	Demands continue for right paper
Gabon	35-40	35-40	35-40	35-40	Some buyers' interests
Madagascar	51-53	51-53	51-53	51-53	Quiet again
Malawi	40-45	40-45	40-45	40-45	Paper needed
Morocco	38-38.5	39.25-39.5	39.25-39.5	36-38	Well offered
Mozambique	4-8	4-8	4-8	4-8	Sleepy again
Niger	29-31	29-31	29-31	29-31	Occasional swap interest
Nigeria	33.1-33.5	34	N/A	34.25-34.75	Restructured/refinanced debt
Senegal	30-33	30-33	30-33	30-33	Uncertain
Sierra Leone	5-8	5-8	5-8	5-8	Dead
Sudan	1-3	1-3	1-3	1-3	No deals yet
Tanzania	15-25	15-25	15-25	15-25	Some interest in trade paper, but deals hard to make
Togo	15-30	15-30	15-30	15-30	Seen nothing; interest still paid late
Uganda	15-30	15-30	15-30	15-30	Price negotiable, buyers selective
Zambia	16-20	16-20	16-20	16-20	Little activity
Zaire	16-18	16-18	16-18	16-18	Local problems mean little appetite

Source: Market data and comments supplied by ANZ merchant bank.

conversion or the buyers in other cases; and the multilateral organizations.

The host-country authorities or the debtor-country authorities, as the case may be, are usually the Ministry of Finance and the Central Bank, but they may also include the Ministry of Trade and the Ministry of Industry. They control the framing of debt-equity (or other conversion) legislation and its implementation typically through a special Debt Conversion Committee within the Central Bank.

The number of creditor banks engaged in swapping debt on the secondary market is significant because of their need to readjust portfolios after the shake-up which came in the aftermath of the excesses of the boom period of developing-country lending in the 1970s. It has been pointed out above that between 30 and 50 per cent of trade in secondary-market debt is done either by 'chain' transactions among commercial bank creditors trying to adjust their portfolios, or by speculators taking positions for yield purposes. Portfolio transactions by bank creditors typically take the form of swapping the debt of countries in which the holder has little specialist acquittance for the debt of countries where it might wish to concentrate its business in order to make optimal use of its expertise. In such cases the debt swap does not result in debt reduction for the debtor, and it may also involve a cash payment between the transactor banks.

Many of the transactor commercial banks, exploiting the expertise they have acquired in trading debt, have set up their own debt-trading teams and offer their services for a fee as brokers. A number of accountancy firms and investment houses also act as brokers. The typical business is to source required types of paper for a potential investor and gather a given amount of eligible debt for debt-equity conversions. This involves a number of 'chain' transactions, exchanging debt A for debt B which in turn is exchanged for debt C plus cash which is used to buy more debt C, which is eligible for debt-equity conversion.

The fourth category of players in the market is the foreign investors or buyers. These *may* be the creditor banks themselves in those rare cases where they take over a local financial intermediary in order to turn it into a branch of their multinational business, but more commonly they are transnational corporations seeking to expand operations in the host country, and taking advantage of the possibility of a front-ended profit, as explained above. Finally, the multilateral organizations are also important players. The IMF's role so far has been relatively limited, although a lobby exists to get it to take a more active role as a partner in a proposed International Debt Facility to buy back debt and pass the gains on to the debtor countries. As for the World Bank, its participation has been somewhat more pronounced through its organs, the International Finance Corporation and the Multilateral Investment Guarantee Agency (MIGA). Both have been active in promoting debt-equity conversion funds, where the local currency raised through conversions is pooled and invested on the local stock market.

Finally, on the issue of fee structure, although there is no hard and fast rule as to what fees are chargeable in a debt-equity conversion deal or in other debt-conversion transactions, including buy-backs, these fees tend to be substantial even though they are negotiable. Orders of magnitude were given in the example cited in the opening section of this chapter, but it is worth noting that even a public multilateral organization such as the IFC, which has recently started to bid routinely against international investment banks for advisory work in less developed countries on account of debt conversion, can charge fees for its services that may run as high as $500–$1,000 per man/day. This fee structure, charged by the corporate finance group in its Capital Markets Division, is significantly more modest than fees charged by IFC's competitors.

Technical and institutional demands on the implementing agency

It is desirable from the outset to give a brief review of what are likely to be the technical and institutional demands on the implementing agencies of debtor countries that may want to carry out formal debt-conversion programmes. For these are considerable, and the fear was expressed by several well-placed experts whom we interviewed, that the costs of setting up these institutions and redeploying the resources to meet the technical demands might outweigh any benefit from conversion, especially in the smaller African countries. At the same time, however, it is conceded that, debt-conversion programme or not, there are aspects of the micro-management of the debt that will, in any case, *have* to be dealt with, so a proportion of the costs will inevitably have to be borne.

Both the institutional and the technical requirements for implementation of a formal debt-conversion programme are complex, and we can hope to survey here only the most obvious ones. Several investment banking units and accounting firms have had experience in designing and installing conversion programmes in a couple of the larger African countries. We interviewed several of them in the first weeks of 1991, and their opinions and judgments, as well as the factual information they supplied, have influenced our assessment and conditioned our analysis. The insight gained from these interviews is reflected not only in this part of the study, but throughout.

The technical requirements of a formal debt-conversion programme are generally the same for all the various types of conversion. They can be classified into two broad categories: those relating to the micro-management of the debt, and those relating to the legal aspect. The technical issues for the micro-management of the debt fall under four headings:

i.   documentation of the original contracts and terms;
ii. breakdown of the debt totals according to creditors;
iii. breakdown of the debt totals according to borrowers and/or purposes;
iv. information processing of secondary-market prices and developments.

It is important, before a debt-conversion transaction can go ahead, to have available the original loan contracts, so that terms can be verified, the degree of fulfilment of obligations ascertained, and provisos studied. These are necessary because any negotiation to reach a new agreement has to be based on the existing contracts. Moreover, the deed for the former obligations has to be legally rescinded before a new one is entered into. The experience of both the relevant staff of UNCTAD (which has a unit providing technical assistance on debt management to several African countries, among others) and the Commonwealth Secretariat's Technical Assistance Group (which provides similar services to member countries of the Commonwealth, among them several African anglophone countries) indicates that quite a number of the smaller African countries still suffer from severe gaps in this micro-management function of their external debt. A few other countries have had their records straightened out commercially at quite significant cost. Both the Commonwealth Secretariat and UNCTAD have done much in recent years, and they also have a long-term technical assistance programme. Nevertheless several African countries still do not have a complete system in place. This is one consideration which those smaller African countries which still do not have an in-house debt-recording and management system in place will have to take into account before deciding on implementing a formal debt-conversion programme. However, ad hoc conversion may necessitate information and original documents only for the specific debt instrument involved. This caveat is not to say that countries that do not have a complete recording system in place should not institute a formal debt programme: it says only that they would need to weigh the costs of setting up a programme against the benefits.

It is also necessary to have a breakdown of the debt total into three important and relevant categories, so as to order priorities. The three categories, according to a breakdown by type of creditor, are as follows:

i. debt owed to official creditors;
ii. uninsured supplier credits;
iii. other commercial bank debt.

With regard to the debt owed to official creditors, the appropriate debt-reduction strategy that African countries should pursue is to seek relief, mostly by write-off. The whole issue is the subject of a complementary study on 'The Efficiency of Debt-

Relief Measures for African Countries'. As for that component of the commercial debt which is insured by the public or para-public Export Credit Guarantee Agencies of the creditor countries, it should not be eligible for debt-equity conversion and buy-backs, because of the limitations on the supply side attendant on the scarce assets to be ceded by the debtor countries. Instead, debt reduction for this component can be pursued by seeking rescheduling over much longer periods, with commensurate grace periods and possibly interest caps.

Of the two remaining categories, it is probable that several countries will find it expedient to reduce the overdue totals on uninsured supplier credits, before tackling other commercial debt. The reason is simply that suppliers, especially of essential imports and of intermediate goods for vital industry, need to be satisfied if supplies are to continue to flow in. The priority is placed on uninsured as opposed to insured supplier credits because the latter have another line of recourse, and the threat of an immediate cut in supply is less intense.

The desirability of having a breakdown of the debt total into these categories points to the necessity, in micro-management of the debt at individual African country level, of keeping proper records of these magnitudes. Therefore, an assessment of the state of management of the external debt in the case of some of the smaller African countries must be made before a full-fledged conversion programme is embarked on. Moreover, the macro-economic situation needs to be enabling, without too volatile inflation, without a grossly overvalued or unstable exchange rate and without too wide a budget or a balance-of-payments deficit, and in the absence of too obvious distortions either in prices or quantities.

Next, for the pricing of the debt, either in negotiated deals or in more competitive conversion mechanisms such as auctions, it is necessary to follow up prices on the secondary 'market' in the large financial centres like London, New York, and Paris. Here, once the investment bankers or other traders on the market are aware that an agent has actually made a deal and has shown interest, information on market developments and prices are supplied basically free over the fax. Fees are charged only for analysis, for the design of conversion schemes, for sourcing and placing, and for actual deals. Nonetheless, in-house staff need to be assigned to the task of studying the data and making the appropriate decisions.

An additional dimension of the technical aspect has to do with the legal issue. Important items to consider in this regard are:

i. 'equal treatment' or '*pari passu*' clauses, generally included in the loan document, whereby if a deal is made with one lender, the same deal must be offered to other lenders in the consortium;

ii. 'new-money' provisos, whenever a debt-conversion deal also seeks to attract new funds from lenders;

iii. creditor-country regulatory measures, especially as they affect the accounting treatment of converted debt and the impact on loan-loss provision and taxes.

Further, and specific to securitization deals, the legal provisions for dealing with the ownership of collateral for collateralized new debt, offered in exchange for old debt, need to be studied. Similarly for debt-equity conversion, company law provisions for management-control procedures when a significant amount of equity is held in foreign hands have to be kept in perspective.

Finally, we turn to analysis of the institutional considerations for debt-conversion programmes. The foremost consideration here relates to the distinction in monetary management methods between the countries of the African Franc-Zone and the others. Debt conversions have significant money-supply impacts on the economy of the country implementing them. African Franc-Zone countries maintain a fixed exchange rate with the French Franc, which is secured almost exclusively through strict control of money-supply movements. We alluded above to the serious difficulties which several countries, including African, that have implemented formal debt-equity programmes, have had with the money-supply impacts. These problems were so severe that a few countries have had to suspend their debt-conversion programmes to quell the fires of monetary pressure. We shall examine this macroeconomic impact in more detail in a later chapter. It remains that, in view of the possible pressures on the exchange rate which could result from excess monetary creation as a consequence of a formal debt-conversion scheme, any African Franc-Zone country wanting to implement a *formal* programme would need the prior approval of the Banque de France and possibly also of the French Treasury. However, it would seem that ad hoc debt conversion has been going on in more than one African Franc-Zone country, especially as a stimulus to the government's privatization programme, and, because the monetary impact is likely to be negligible, the question of seeking Banque de France approval has so far not arisen.

Other institutional requirements specific to debt-equity conversion programmes include:

i.   the setting up of an investment screening unit to determine which projects are on priority lists to benefit from debt-equity conversion incentives;
ii. the setting up of a monitoring unit to track the use of the local-currency proceeds of debt conversion, and for administering blocked accounts;[10]
iii. the building-up of extra analytical capacity to assess the economy-wide impact of debt conversion via the monetary and fiscal processes;
iv. the choice of a pricing system for conversion, the alternative being an auction mechanism or other administrative system, plus the determination of commissions.

Similar institutional requirements exist for debt-debt swaps and debt buy-back mechanisms. For the debt-debt mechanism one needs to set up a debt-conversion unit for selecting the types of new debts to issue and the type of collateral to offer. A monitoring and approval unit would also be needed if the debt-debt swap took the form of onlending. Debt-in-kind swaps would mostly be done ad hoc.

The essential point to bear in mind is that African countries contemplating installing formal debt-conversion programmes need at the minimum to address the technical, legal and institutional issues raised in this section.

---

[10] For a more elaborate discussion, see the opening section of this chapter.

3

The Practice of Debt Conversion in Important Implementing Countries

It is important that any African country contemplating the implementation of a formal debt-equity or other debt-conversion programme should derive as many lessons as possible from the experience of other countries that have gone through the process. Accordingly, this chapter offers a very brief description of the programmes of Mexico, Chile, Jamaica, the Philippines and Nigeria, each country having been chosen because of its particular relevance. Mexico's programme resulted in a significant turnaround in direct foreign investment, Chile's programme is widely regarded as the most successful debt-equity scheme overall, Jamaica's programme is one of the rare schemes to be instituted by a small country, while the Philippines' programme offers an Asian example.[1] Nigeria's programme is the most prominent African case. More detailed, readily available information about these programmes can be obtained from the UNCTC/SELA Guide and two other widely-circulated publications: The Economist Publications' *Guide to Debt Equity Swaps (1987)*[2] and Euromoney's *Special Report: PW/Euromoney Debt-Equity Swap Guide (1988)*.

Mexico

Mexico's programme is one of the better structured both in terms of its investment-related and of its financial aspects. With regard to the former, emphasis is placed on providing elaborate details on explicit investment priorities and on the acceptable uses contemplated for the conversion proceeds, and defining eligible investors as well as ratifying the appropriate legislation on foreign investment. Originally open only to foreign investors who were not residents of Mexico or who did not have their main place of business there, the programme was subsequently opened to nationals with regard to its debt capitalization elements. The originally restrictive foreign investment law was subsequently liberalized in the context of opening up the country to more competition and integrating it into the international economy, so that, while investment through debt-equity conversion is voted by the National Commission on Foreign Investment, it is now done within a liberal framework. Preference in the debt-equity conversion programme is given to privatizations and to investments that concern exports, to the implementation of increased productive capacity, to the transfer of new technology, and to

[1] Experiences of debt conversion other than for debt-equity swaps will be referred to, passim, in subsequent chapters. The important experience of Bolivia in significantly reducing its debt through buy-back and debt-equity conversion will also be analysed.

[2] Special Report No 1104 by Steven M. Rubin (London: Economist Publications, September, 1987).

investments that will increase national content levels. Various graded categories are defined with correspondingly attractive incentives offered. In terms of the acceptable uses of the proceeds, the programme permits both equity acquisitions (*new* and existing) and the payment of local debt, while conversion funds, pooling proceeds for investment, are in an incipient stage. Importantly, the Mexican debt-equity programme does not require matching funds for investment, and the only special restriction on the remittance of profits is that for five years they not exceed the corresponding interest payments which they replace. Capital cannot be repatriated for 12 years. Overall these conditions make the Mexican programme a very liberal one.

Regarding the financial aspect of the programme, the focus has been less on reduction of the debt through the capture of a portion of the discount in the secondary market than on attracting additional investment to be channelled to priority areas. Originally, the rate of exchange used was the higher parallel market rate rather than the official rate, and administrative fees were minimal. The purpose was to encourage the investor rather than to generate revenue, and graduated discounts were used only to make the priority order of investments effective. Yearly quotas were set for conversion, to keep the programme manageable and to avoid stoking inflation, but the auction mechanism used to regulate access to the quotas laid greater emphasis on priority of investment rather than the size of the discount. Certain administrative safeguards were imposed, such as unlimited auditing of the companies receiving the investment and the disbursing of local currency directly to the recipients' national suppliers, contractors or creditors, to ensure *bona fide* investment and to guarantee maximum success in the goals set.

Mexico's debt-equity conversion programme has been very successful in resuscitating direct foreign investment to levels that exceed the 1980–81 boom in foreign capital inflows. Conversions are reported to have accounted for over 60 per cent of direct foreign investment during the crisis period, although debt reduction amounted to only 7 per cent of outstanding transnational bank debt. In addition, the investments went heavily into priority areas as defined by the government. Finally, a significant portion of the investment went into big projects.

Chile

Unlike that of Mexico, Chile's general debt-conversion programme (including, but not restricted to, debt-equity conversion) was designed mainly to help in reducing the debt and debt-service burden. As such, other debt-conversion instruments, aside from debt-equity, played an important role, and together they managed, over a period of five years, to reduce Chile's debt by almost a half of the medium and long-term debt stock, at a value of over $8 billion. The Chilean programme uses three important tools. The first (referred to as Chapter 18 of the Compendium of Rules on International Exchange) aims at encouraging the return of flight capital, and allows eligible debt to be exchanged for local currency on a no-questions-asked basis. The Chilean national (resident abroad or in Chile) is in effect granted an amnesty on having illegally transferred funds abroad in the past. He is encouraged to bring back his capital for domestic investment or other purposes by being permitted to cash-in on the discount offered on debt bought in the secondary market, but he is denied subsequent access to foreign exchange to transfer profits or capital since he is not treated as a foreign investor.

The second tool is referred to as Chapter 19 of the same compendium of Rules. This offers the same type of special advantages to foreigners, and to Chilean nationals resident and domiciled abroad, to convert purchased debt to local currency for investment in priority projects, as does the Mexican programme. Subsequently, after a defined remittance-prohibition period, they become entitled to obtain access to foreign exchange for dividend or profit remittances in a fashion similar to normal foreign investment. The incentive to the investor, as in the Mexican case, is the front-ended profit by way of the purchase of the debt on the secondary market. The capitalization of Chilean investment companies operating conversion funds (the pooling of proceeds from debt conversion for purposes of equity investment) managed by a holding company is also permitted under Chapter 19. The third tool is a package of debt-conversion mechanisms, essentially of the debt-debt swap types described above, including re-lending, onlending or direct buy-back. In general, each tool has succeeded in bringing about approximately one-third of the total $8 bn. reduction in Chilean debt.

The Chilean programme is generally considered the most flexible of all the operating programmes. More than a couple of the half dozen investment or merchant bankers we interviewed were of the opinion that its success was due precisely to this flexibility, and they recommended that any African country hoping to implement a new debt-conversion programme would do well to seek inspiration from the Chilean programme. Chile's foreign investment statute is also quite liberal and the investment climate, unencumbered by a lot of restrictions, is considered by major market participants to be a crucial factor in the degree of success of any debt-equity conversion programme. The Chilean programme does not set hard and fast rules on the acceptability of investments, on investment priorities or on the ethical question of granting amnesty to former capital flight perpetrators. On the other hand, the Chilean authorities maintain that the confirmation of the true identity of the foreign investor, and the strict monitoring of the permitted use of proceeds, are among the most rigorous examinations performed by the Central Bank.[3]

While the Chilean programme is light on investment-related restrictions (allowing new equity investment, the purchase of existing assets, and participation in government privatization operations, with priorities implicit but not mandatory), it clearly establishes and enforces its financial aspects. Effort is not spared, albeit in somewhat subtler ways than through auctions, to capture a good portion of the discount on the secondary market.

---

[3]However, critics still maintain that the authorities have been obliged to turn a blind eye to camouflaged Chilean investors because of the otherwise unfair advantage given to foreigners.

Valuation of the debt for conversion is always at less than 100 per cent of face-value, and the proceeds payable come in two possible forms: either notes to bearer are issued by the Central Bank denominated in US dollars and payable in local currency, maturing over 10 years with the LIBOR rate of interest plus a very marginal spread, or negotiable bearer instruments are issued by the Central Bank denominated in the local inflation-index unit, with a maturity of 15 years bearing interest. In practical terms, these provisos translate into the fact that the bonds issued by the Central Bank have a present value of around 92 per cent of face-value and, once exchanged in the local financial market, usually produce an 88 per cent face-value in local currency for the investor. Consequently the Central Bank takes a profit of 8 per cent of face-value, while the local financial market takes another 4 per cent.

While the Chilean programme has no doubt been quite successful in reducing the stock of debt, as mentioned above, and has further permitted external economic performance to improve in the sense that it has helped revive foreign direct investment and enabled punctual servicing of the reduced debt, it has not translated into a return to voluntary lending by the international capital market. This is the bottom-line by which the ex-chief negotiator for Chile, Hermon Somerwille,[4] himself seemed to be judging the degree of success of the programme when he complained to *Euromoney* (September 1987): 'We have paid the interest due punctually. We have complied with every issue . . . we have handled private sector issues. . . . I think a country like ours should get the rewards of the market place.'

An additional problem with the Chilean programme is that the debt-equity conversion operations have taken on a highly speculative nature, so that the narrow interests of the banks seem to override the broader interests of the country. These considerations, plus the complete absence in African countries of domestic capital markets anywhere as sophisticated as that of Chile, should be borne in mind before endorsing the advice, offered to us by the investment bankers we interviewed, that African

---

[4]Quoted in the UNCTC/SELA *Guide for Decision-Makers*, op. cit., p. 85.

countries contemplating instituting debt-equity conversion schemes should model them on Chile's programme.

Jamaica

Jamaica's debt-conversion programme is modest in its aspirations in that it aims to convert no more than $185 m., or only 6 per cent of its total debt of $3.5 bn, and it is designed explicitly as a tool to revive foreign investment rather than to reduce the debt. Since debt reduction is not the primary aim, the return of flight capital is not pursued and, as a consequence, participation in the programme is restricted to non-residents, though not necessarily to non-nationals. This makes it possible for the large number of Jamaicans resident in the United States and the United Kingdom to invest back in the home country and take in the benefits by way of discount on the secondary debt market, on an equal footing with other foreign investors. Finally, the programme is closely tied to the government's privatization programme.

The programme is quite straightforward in implementation. Determinedly pursuing the foreign-investment revival goal, it contains a clause providing for the possibility of a case-by-case matching funds requirement for the investor to bring in new money in addition to the conversion proceeds. It is non-restrictive as regards eligibility of investment projects, although the tourism sector, the export-processing zone and export-oriented and labour-intensive projects are favoured. The Central Bank, which implements the programme, reserves the right to charge a fee that may go up to 10 per cent, and redemption is made not in cash but in equity investment bonds that can be discounted with local financial institutions to raise the local currency requirements of approved projects. Dividend remittances cannot occur within three years and capital repatriation cannot be made within seven years.

The Jamaican debt-conversion programme is generally considered to have been a disappointment. Deals made have been small and it is estimated that no more than $30 m. of foreign debt has so far been swapped, in spite of the significant potential saving of up to 50 per cent to investors. Two reasons can be advanced for the failure: political instability and the holding-back game of bank creditors who hold the larger part of the debt.

Philippines

The Philippine debt-conversion programme is of special interest because a central specific feature is the use of conversion funds. These utilize transnational bank debt transformed into special series Central Bank bills to purchase shares in Philippine enterprises through authorized investment operations. These funds are closed-ended, which means that they cannot be withdrawn, and they are usually liquidated after ten years. Dividends are reinvested until the liquidation date. A not insignificant amount of $125 m. of external debt has been converted through conversion funds.

A second facet of the Philippine programme is the direct debt-equity conversion scheme, and this is considerably more important. It aims not only to provide incentives for direct foreign investment but also to encourage the return of flight capital. The programme did not spurn the possibility of capturing a part of the discount on the secondary debt market, so reduction of the debt was also a consideration. However, the investment aspect of the programme was of greater concern, and an explicit list of priority investments was drawn up. High on this list were projects that involved export-oriented manufacturing activity, the processing of agricultural output especially if intended for export, the provision of health care services or the construction of health care facilities locally, the construction of low-and middle-income housing projects locally, as well as the construction of local educational facilities. Later the list was expanded to include banking and financial services. Eligible investors include both foreigners and Filipinos, the latter not being entitled to subsequent access to foreign exchange for profit or capital remittance purposes. The accepted uses of the proceeds include purchase by the recipient company of new capital equipment or tangible goods necessary for an expansion of activity and the construction of expanded plant capacity, but exclude the purchase of existing assets or shares of a Philippine company. Uses for portfolio investment, for working capital and for the repayment of local-currency obligations of the Philippine recipient company are also disallowed. Restrictions on capital repatriation are for three years in the case of preferred investment and five years for other investments. Restrictions on profits remittances apply only to the other investments category and are for four years. It is noteworthy that private-sector trade debt is not eligible for conversion.

Regarding the programme's financial aspects, the fee structure for conversion has been modified from 10 per cent of the local-currency value of the investment to a graduated scale which runs from 8 per cent to 24 per cent depending on whether the fresh-money requirements are as high as 60 per cent or as low as zero. The scale is slightly lower for priority investments. For the year 1988, there was an informal $180 m. limit placed on debt conversion using Central Bank paper. Allocation of quotas is based on a points system for investment projects, depending on foreign-exchange generation capacity, labour-intensiveness and geographical location of the project.

The Philippine programme is regarded as having been quite successful. It is estimated to have generated over $624 m. of approved investment by 1988, most of it during that year. It seems that the demand for debt paper outstrips supply. A good amount of flight capital repatriation is also estimated to have occurred, but this remains difficult to quantify and to separate from purely direct foreign investment.

Nigeria

The Nigerian Debt Conversion Programme, established in July 1988 as part of the government's efforts to reduce the burden of the external debt on the economy, had the additional aim of appropriating to the economy part of the discount at which Nigerian paper was being traded on the secondary market. The Debt Conversion Committee, which is charged with the responsibility of designing and implementing an efficient debt-conversion programme by establishing clear and precise approval criteria and procedures, by reviewing and approving applications and transactions, and by monitoring progress and reviewing procedures on a continuous basis, is chaired by the Governor of the Central Bank of Nigeria. The other members are all at ministerial level, including the Ministers of Finance, of Planning, of Industry, and of Justice as well as the Secretary to the Federal Government. The Secretariat is provided by the Central Bank. The highlights of the Nigerian Debt Conversion Programme are its objectives, the types of debt eligible for conversion, the eligible transactions, the eligible participants, the mode of conversion and the restrictions on remittances.

The explicit objectives of the programme are:

i. to improve Nigeria's external debt position by reducing the stock of foreign-currency denominated debt in order to alleviate the debt-service burden;
ii. to improve the economic environment and render it more attractive to foreign investors;
iii. to serve as an additional incentive for the repatriation of flight capital;
iv. to stimulate employment-generating investments in industries with significant dependence on local inputs;
v. to encourage the creation and development of export-oriented industries, thereby diversifying the export base of the economy;
vi. to increase access to appropriate technology and external markets, and to derive other benefits associated with foreign investment.

The debts eligible for conversion under the programme were initially limited to promissory notes issued in 1984 following that year's major debt-rationalizing exercise. Subsequently, eligibility was extended to promissory notes issued by the Federal Ministry of Finance as well as restructured and refinanced debt having a maturity of over one year owed to international commercial banks. The larger part of the promissory notes had originated from debt owed to suppliers.

Four categories of eligible transactions are allowed under the programme. These are:

i. conversion into cash for the purpose of making a gift/grant to Nigerian non-profit-making entities such as educational institutions, research centres, charitable organizations, religious bodies, benevolent trusts and foundations;
ii. conversion for the acquisition of naira-denominated debt instruments issued by the Central Bank of Nigeria, such as naira notes, development stocks and other local instruments designated specifically for the programme;
iii. conversion into equity, preference shares, debentures and loan stocks of existing companies for the purpose of expansion or recapitalization of existing projects;
iv. conversion for investment in completely new projects.

All holders or assignees of designated debt, both Nigerians and foreigners, whether corporate bodies or individuals, resident or non-resident, are eligible to participate in the programme, provided that the foreign exchange required for the purchase of the foreign debt instrument from the original holders satisfies origin requirements. These require that the foreign exchange should originate from abroad and is not from foreign exchange purchased in the Nigerian foreign-exchange market or from export proceeds. In addition, the enterprises to be financed with the conversion proceeds have to be registered under existing Nigerian company law at the time of the transaction.

The mode of conversion, including the discount offered as a percentage of the face-value of the debt to be redeemed, is by auction, although the Debt Conversion Committee may at its discretion approve an application for conversion outside the auction. In cases where the latter mode is used, conversion is effected at a price determined by the weighted average of discounts offered by successful bidders at the most recent auction.

The regulations contain provisos for restrictions on remittances under the programme. Interest and profits and dividends arising from the activity of enterprises financed by conversion proceeds are not repatriable for five years. The initial capital, or proceeds arising from the sale of equity thus acquired, cannot be repatriated within 10 years subsequent to the initial investment. Annual repatriation of capital after these 10 years is limited to 20 per cent.

The conversion procedure itself starts with the investor identifying the project within the eligible transactions categories, and obtaining the consent of the company to buy-in if it is a portfolio investment, or incorporating his company if he is setting up a new one. Then he secures approval in principle from the Committee through the Secretariat at the Central Bank. At the auction, the investor's bid, including the amount of debt to be redeemed and the discount offered, is considered together with the applications of other investors through conversion, and the bids are ranked in decreasing order of discounts offered. Permission to redeem is given by discount rank until the amount previously fixed by the Debt Conversion Committee for redemption is exhausted. The Committee may set a reserve price (the minimum discount) above which no conversion will be effected at any auction.

The redemptor then surrenders the debt instrument to the Central Bank, which forwards it for cancellation. A transaction commission of 2.5 per cent on the discounted value of the debt cancelled is also paid to the Central Bank, in foreign exchange. Thereafter, the Central Bank pays the naira proceeds into the redemptor's blocked account at the Central Bank of Nigeria, and disbursements are paid only after staff of the Secretariat have visited the site of the project and identified the immediate cash needs. Subsequently, on satisfying the staff about additional cash needs, further funds are released to the designated commercial bank account of the beneficiary.

The programme builds in certain safeguards to deal with problems that have been identified as inherent in debt-conversion programmes. Four of these problems are: possible adverse effects on the balance of payments, stimulating inflation, 'round-tripping', and the diversion of funds to uses other than those approved. The inbuilt mechanism guarding against an adverse effect on the balance of payments is the requirement that residents who participate in the programme source the foreign exchange utilized to purchase the debt from outside the country and not from export proceeds. To forestall any stimulus to inflation, the Committee has set, and constantly reviews, ceilings on the amount of conversion to be done in each period; it also ensures that the injection of conversion proceeds is in line with the monetary, credit and other macroeconomic objectives of the government. Further, the fact that the proceeds immediately go into a blocked account and are released only gradually also helps contain the inflationary stimulus. Thirdly, 'round-tripping' is the pernicious practice whereby local exporters are tempted, by the possibilities of gain offered by the debt-conversion mechanism, to retain a part of their foreign-currency proceeds to buy back debt at a discount, redeem it in local currency often at a premium over normal exchange rates, and buy back foreign currency on the parallel market, either to fulfil remittance requirements or, worse, if they can get away with it, to restart the process all over again. To reduce this problem of round-tripping, the Nigerian programme provides that the proceeds of conversion shall be used exclusively to finance local costs of projects, while all off-shore costs are financed by the redemptor from foreign exchange sourced abroad. Furthermore, all designated debt-conversion accounts are refused access to Nigeria's foreign-exchange market without prior approval, and information is required to be lodged monthly by enterprises benefiting from conversion-proceeds investment about all their imports and foreign-exchange trans-actions. Finally, to prevent diversification of funds to unauthorized uses, developments in approved projects are closely monitored.

The performance of the Nigerian programme indicates a substantial measure of success, with the approval rate showing a significant amount of debt reduction in the pipeline, and the management of the impact on the macroeconomy of the redemption already achieved proving quite effective. Between August 1988 and December 1990, the Nigerian programme received 206 debt conversion applications for a total amount of $3.24 bn. The largest number of applications, worth over half the total in value, was received in 1988, while a somewhat smaller amount in value, with commensurately fewer applications, was received in 1990. (The value of applications in 1989 were one-tenth of the three-year total.) Of the amount of $3.24 bn for the period 1988–90, one-fifth of the applications worth $1.23 bn was for agriculture and agro-allied projects, one-half worth $677 m. was for manufacturing, 6 projects worth $317 m. were for hotels and tourism, and the considerable number of 18 applications worth $237 m. was for cash gifts and grants, while an additional 17 applications worth $674 m. were for the acquisition of government securities and shares of publicly-quoted enterprises. The significant number of 37 applications worth $718 m. were made by Nigerians.

The Debt Conversion Committee granted approval in principle to 153 applications with a total value of $1,524 m. Of these, 39 applications worth $312 m. were for agriculture, 86 worth $542 m. were for manufacturing, 6 worth $275 m. were for hotels and tourism, 11 worth $133 m. were for gifts and grants, and 3 worth $154 m. were for investment in government securities.

The number of auctions held between August 1988 and December 1990 amounted to 16 with the average amount actually redeemed per session being $26.6 m. The average discounted amount redeemed was equal to $14.2 m., making the effective discount, calculated on this basis, 46.6 per cent. The range of actual discounts was from 40.7 per cent to 52.9 per cent, with the highest discount offer at 58 per cent. In October 1990, having reached the ceiling on conversion it had planned for the year 1990, the Debt Conversion Committee temporarily suspended further auctions under the programme. The Central Bank was also at that time taking measures to mop up the excess liquidity in the economy, and the Committee's decision was aimed at aligning the programme with government objectives. The programme was resumed in early 1991, and three auctions had been held by mid-year 1991.

It is also noteworthy that a small number of conversions were made, with the approval of the Committee, outside the auction system. An amount of $150 m. covering 14 transactions at an average discount of 49.6 per cent had been converted in this way by end-1990.

The amount of debt actually cancelled between August 1988 and December 1990 totalled $514 m. (out of a total $1,524 m. for which approval in principle had been given). The sum of $246.6 m. was thus appropriated to the economy in the form of discounts offered by the redemptors. Promissory notes accounted for the bulk of the debt redeemed at $341.6 m. or 66.5 per cent. The rest was bank debt, which only became eligible in November 1989.

The impact of Nigeria's programme on the economy has been quite beneficial, while possible adverse side-effects, such as a stimulus to inflation, round-tripping, possible encouragement of the parallel foreign exchange market, and loss of control of key sectors of the economy to foreigners, have been avoided. On the debt reduction side proper, Nigeria's external liabilities had been thus reduced by $514 m. with commensurate reduction in debt service, which amounts to a positive impact on the balance of payments. In addition, in so far as additional foreign investment funds were brought in to supplement the conversion proceeds and channelled into new projects or expansions, the capital account of the balance of payments also benefited. With a significant amount of the projects financed by conversion proceeds in the manufacturing sector being export-oriented, the current account of the balance of payments is also estimated to have been helped.

On the domestic scene, productive capacity and employment have both benefited from the additional investment, and this benefit was enhanced by the fact that these investments were channelled to priority sectors, thus ensuring an efficient allocation of resources. The direct addition to employment creation has been estimated at around nine thousand, with numerous additional indirect employment opportunities created. The rate of utilization of installed capacity by the beneficiary companies is estimated to have increased by 21 per cent. The transfer of new technology also seems to have been significant, with several specific cases of new or improved processes and techniques being reported and verified, both in the manufacturing and the agricultural sectors. Furthermore, the significant amounts converted for use in gifts and grants have improved donations to universities, paramedical organizations and welfare institutions, all contributing to social improvement. The safeguards, taken to make the approval process efficient, to monitor disbursements, to track the sourcing of foreign exchange, and to put ceilings on amounts converted have helped considerably in avoiding the problems of losing control of sectors of the economy to foreigners, of round-tripping, and of inflation. The repatriation of flight capital has also been significantly helped. The possibility of pressures from these problem areas building up always remains present, however, and the Secretariat staff is constantly vigilant in reviewing developments. With these caveats, the Nigerian programme has demonstrated that, for a well designated debt-conversion programme, and provided the enabling macroeconomic environment is in place, the potential for deriving significant benefits is very real.

4

The Scope for Market-Based Debt Reduction in African Countries

It is important, when assessing the scope for debt conversion in African countries, to keep in view which of the various conversion mechanisms already described one is referring to. The present chapter considers only two major types of conversion: the debt-equity swap and the self-financed debt buy-back. The scope for debt conversion through other mechanisms such as securitization and third-party-financed buy-backs, is analysed in a later chapter which considers all aspects of alternative conversion mechanisms.

The scope for debt conversion through the mechanism of the

debt-equity swap can be gauged by assessing, on the one hand, the nature and quantity of financial paper likely to be offered by holders of African countries' debt instruments, and, on the other hand, the nature of the counterpart assets (equity in existing or new ventures) to be ceded by the African countries. These correspond, respectively, to the demand side for debt conversion, and the supply side. When the reference is to the self-financed buy-back, the demand side is still measured by the nature and quantity of financial paper offered by creditors, while the supply side turns on the prospects of the African debtors having available or being able to build up excess reserves to buy back the debt. The structure of this chapter, therefore, follows the line of analysing separately, in the case of each of the two conversion mechanisms identified, the demand side and the supply side, in order to bring out the elements determining the scope for debt conversion to reduce the debt burden and/or to achieve one or more of the subsidiary goals identified in Chapter I, such as catalyzing new investment, encouraging privatization or stimulating technology transfer.

The demand side:
the nature of financial paper offered

It has already been pointed out that the transactions that have taken place so far on the secondary market for African countries' debt indicate that only a very small fraction of the total stock of financial paper held by creditors has actually come on to the market. In particular, the cumulative volume of African debt paper traded during the four-year period 1986-9 at a total $800 m. of final transactions amounts to only 1.3 per cent of the estimated $61 bn commercial debt stock outstanding which is eligible for conversion.[1] If we were to go exclusively by this measure, we would immediately conclude that, from the demand side alone, the scope for debt-equity and debt buy-back

[1]See Table IV.1 below and the discussion later in this chapter.

operations to reduce Africa's external debt is very marginal indeed. At the same time, however, it is equally erroneous, as has already been pointed out, to assume that the totality of the outstanding debt stock is on offer by creditors at the prices on the secondary market. The reality is somewhat more complex than that, as it is, indeed, for the concept of a demand *schedule* as opposed to the naive idea of quantity demanded.

There are various groups of creditors. These are commercial banks who are original holders of the debt, commercial banks who have sold part of their debt on the secondary market to would-be individual or corporate investors, suppliers who have extended short- and medium-term credit to the debtor countries outside the scope of their countries' export credit guarantee agencies, and suppliers in creditor countries who have extended guaranteed credit under their countries' procurement-tied aid. The amounts of financial paper on offer from each group of creditor will vary according to the type of creditor. They will also vary according to the type of conversion mechanism envisaged.

With regard to creditor types, it needs to be stated from the start that the commercial banks are *not*, at the moment, very keen to offer their financial paper for debt-equity swap operations. Several reasons were offered to us by our interviewees to explain this position. In the first instance, the legislation of the countries where some banks have their headquarters do not allow, or at best limit, their participation in equity ownership of non-financial ventures. This is the case, notably, for US commercial banks where the regulatory principles make a distinction between banking activity and non-banking commercial activity. Banking regulations require that prior approval be secured before investment in non-financial-service ventures is made. Application of these prior-approval regulations points to a rule-of-thumb guideline that approval almost invariably limits banks to investments below $15 m. or 20 per cent of the voting shares, whichever is the higher. Moreover, the holding period of an investment in non-financial businesses is limited to a certain number of years, which is sometimes a constraining factor. These considerations essentially withdraw from the quantum of outstanding debt that can be considered as eligible for debt-equity conversion, all debt owed to US-based commercial banks.

In the second instance, even where the legislation is more liberal in such matters – as would be the case for British and other European banks – the banks themselves are averse to engaging in equity participation to any significant degree, because they feel they lack expertise in such business and are not ready to set up new units to develop such expertise. Moreover, possibilities of conflict of interest are very real, as when credit allocation denies funds to a venture because of its performance, even though the credit-extending agency happens to be the same bank that has a minority equity stake in the venture. Finally, banks feel that there is no advantage for them in undertaking such equity participation since the absence of capital markets in practically all of the indebted African countries means that they cannot sell their shares even in the medium term, while the disadvantage is very real. This is in contrast to the considerations of merchant banks or multinational manufacturing firms, which do have possibilities of capital gains. However, a significant amount of what was originally commercial bank debt will, at any one time, have been bought on the secondary market by individual or corporate would-be investors. This commercial bank debt is the most important source of demand for debt-equity swaps.

Still in the context of restrictions from the perspective of creditor types, the long-term non-bank trade claims on African indebted countries consist largely of procurement-tied bilateral credit extended by Paris Club creditors through their export credit guarantee agencies. These are doubly ineligible for conversion. Firstly, the debtor African country would classify such debt at a lower level of priority of consideration for conversion, because it is guaranteed and therefore the pressure to repay is less intense. Secondly, the Paris Club itself has so far not allowed the holders of these claims to offer them on the market for debt-equity conversion operations. As a consequence, a quite significant proportion – over two-thirds – of the total commercial debt stock lies outside the range of debt eligible for conversion. Roughly, then, these considerations would leave, for the whole of Africa, an amount of $61.6 bn at the most of financial paper claims against African debtors that would be forthcoming on offer in the secondary market at a sufficiently high price. The breakdown of this total, for Africa as a whole and for individual African countries, is given in Table IV.1.

Next, there is the impact of the price on the quantity of financial paper offered on the secondary market. At one end of the spectrum is the hard reality that if one were, for example, to have gone out to buy the entire stock of commercial debt of Côte d'Ivoire at the prevailing price in mid-January 1991 of 3 to 4 per cent on the dollar, one would have been very disappointed to find that very little was on offer. What is more, the price would have been likely to shoot up dramatically as a result of the attempt to purchase, as demonstrated in Chapter 2. At the other end of the spectrum is the theoretical possibility, analysed in the Appendix, of prices adjusting instantaneously in a fully competitive fashion, so that the entire stock of commercial debt *does* come on offer on the market, but at a price which makes the transaction totally unappealing to the debt-holder, whether he envisages a debt-equity swap, a buy-back or some other conversion procedure. By far the most common situation lies somewhere between these two extremes. Adjustment in prices and in quantities offered is imperfect. There *does* emerge some sort of a 'demand schedule', but of an irregular shape. Typically, where market prices are in the range of 20 to 40 per cent, there is likely to be some elasticity in the curve, with anywhere between 30 and 70 per cent of the financial paper on offer or ready to become so. Outside this range, at the lower end, there would probably be no more than 2 to 3 per cent of the eligible financial paper on offer at any one time. At the upper end, while all the paper would theoretically be on offer, there would be no market, since the debtor or any other transactor would not be ready to buy. Such would be the case for Zimbabwe paper which is not of 'blocked dividend' origin, or for Mauritius paper or the debt instruments of other well-performing countries, for which the price would be 100 cents on the dollar or nearly so.

The amount of financial paper on offer also varies according to the type of conversion operation envisaged. So far in this section, the discussion of the demand side for conversion has

Table IV.1   Possible total commercial debt eligible for reduction at end December 1989 (US$m.)

Country	Short-term non-guaranteed bank claims	Long-term non-guaranteed bank claims	Eligible total
Algeria	2,519	10,632	13,151
Angola	437	426	863
Benin	33	50	83
Botswana	14	–	14
Burkina Faso	43	15	58
Burundi	8	6	14
Cameroon	350	619	2,130
Central African Rep.	15	6	21
Chad	15	–	15
Congo	680	935	1,615
Côte d'Ivoire	2,611	1,346	3,957
Egypt	7,464	1,905	9,369
Equatorial Guinea	2	10	12
Ethiopia	57	46	103
Gabon	533	526	1,059
Gambia	7	19	26
Ghana	93	–	93
Guinea	81	52	133
Guinea-Bissau	9	31	40
Kenya	578	525	1,103
Lesotho	15	1	16
Liberia	119	151	270
Libya	1,859	–	1,859
Madagascar	59	41	100
Malawi	29	35	64
Mali	59	15	74
Mauritania	108	21	336
Mauritius	17	57	74
Morocco	895	3,162	4,057
Mozambique	207	80	287
Niger	164	328	492
Nigeria	2,538	10,621	13,159
Rwanda	29	9	38
Sao Tome & Principe	3	2	5
Senegal	579	216	795
Sierra Leone	92	22	114
Somalia	71	20	91
Sudan	711	813	1,524
Swaziland	17	13	30
Tanzania	729	25	754

Table IV.1 *Continued*

Country	Short-term non-guaranteed bank claims	Long-term non-guaranteed bank claims	Eligible total
Togo	128	59	187
Tunisia	1,223	651	1,874
Uganda	46	24	70
Zaire	554	603	1,157
Zambia	623	195	818
Zimbabwe	362	481	843
AFRICA	26,785	34,781	61,566

Source: Compiled from OECD/BIS: *Statistics on External Indebtedness*. (half-yearly) January 1991, and World Bank: *World Debt Tables* 1989/90.

been carried on without making explicit whether it is a debt-equity operation that is envisaged or a self-financed buy-back, because certain of the considerations of transactors are common to both. But other considerations are different for each type. In addition, within the single category of debt-equity conversion, different mechanisms may carry different incentives and, depending on the degree of their attractiveness, the quantity on offer can be greater or less. But this is a factor that more properly belongs to the supply side of debt conversion. The demand side depends more on the *perception* of investment opportunities and on opportunities for profit and capital gain by the debt-instrument holders.

An approximate idea of the complex factors, in addition to the existing local presence, which would guide a would-be investor in assessing the business and profit opportunities in a debtor country that is implementing a debt-equity conversion pro-gramme, can be obtained from studying Tables IV.2 to IV.4. Certainly, the basic economic indicators of the debtor country are a prime consideration. These would include its population, its GNP per capita, its recent growth performance in GNP, its average annual inflation rate, the extent of urbanization of its labour force, and other factors about its infrastructure and the quality of the labour force. These, apart from the last two, are presented in Table IV.2 for each individual African country. Beyond these factors, however, the structure of production in

Table IV.2 Basic indicators of African countries: 1988

Country	Population (millions) mid-1988	GNP per capita $ 1988	Av. growth rate of GNP 1965–88 %	Av. annual inflation rate 1980–88 %	(Urban population as % of total) urbanisation
Algeria	23.8	2,360	2.7	4.4	44
Angola	9.4	N/A	N/A	N/A	27
Benin	4.4	390	0.1	8.0	40
Botswana	1.2	1,010	8.6	10.0	22
Burkina Faso	8.5	210	1.2	3.2	9
Burundi	5.1	240	3.0	4.0	7
Cameroon	11.2	1,010	3.7	7.0	47
Cent. Afr. Rep.	2.9	380	−0.5	6.7	45
Chad	5.4	160	−2.0	3.2	31
Congo	2.1	910	3.5	0.8	41
Côte d'Ivoire	11.2	770	0.9	3.8	45
Egypt	50.2	660	3.6	10.6	48
Equatorial Guinea					
Ethiopia	47.4	120	−0.1	2.1	13
Gabon	1.1	2,970	0.9	0.9	44
Gambia					
Ghana	14.0	400	−1.6	46.1	33
Guinea	5.4	430	N/A	N/A	24
Guinea-Bissau					
Kenya	22.4	370	1.9	9.6	22
Lesotho	1.7	420	5.2	12.2	19

Liberia	2.4	N/A	N/A	N/A	43
Libya	4.2	5,420	-2.7	0.1	68
Madagascar	10.9	190	-1.8	17.3	24
Malawi	8.0	170	1.1	12.6	14
Mali	8.0	230	1.6	3.7	19
Mauritania	1.9	480	-0.4	9.4	40
Mauritius	1.1	1,800	2.9	7.8	42
Morocco	24	830	2.3	7.7	47
Mozambique	14.9	100		33.6	24
Niger	7.3	300	-2.3	3.6	18
Nigeria	110.1	290	0.9	11.6	34
Rwanda	6.7	320	1.5	4.1	7
Sao Tome & Principe					
Senegal	7.0	650	-0.8	8.1	38
Sierra Leone	3.9	N/A	N/A	N/A	26
Somalia	5.9	170	0.5	38.4	37
Sudan	23.8	480	0.0	33.5	21
Swaziland					
Tanzania	24.7	160	-0.5	25.7	30
Togo	3.4	370	0.0	6.1	25
Tunisia	7.8	1,230	3.4	7.7	54
Uganda	16.2	280	-3.1	100.7	10
Zaire	33.4	170	-2.1	56.1	39
Zambia	7.6	290	-2.1	33.5	54
Zimbabwe	9.3	650	1.0	12.1	27

Source: World Development Report 1990: Washington DC: World Bank.

Table IV.3 The structure of production in African countries: 1988. Distribution of GDP (%)

Country	GDP (US$m.)	Agriculture	Industry	Manufacturing	Services
Algeria	51,900	13	43	(12)	44
Angola					
Benin	1,710	40	13	(6)	47
Botswana	1,940	3	55	(5)	42
Burkina Faso	1,750	39	23	(13)	38
Burundi	960	56	15	(10)	29
Cameroon	12,900	26	30	(13)	44
Cent. Afr. Rep.	1,080	44	12	(8)	44
Chad	920	47	18	(15)	35
Congo	2,150	15	30	(8)	54
Côte d'Ivoire	7,650	36	25	(16)	39
Egypt	34,330	21	25	(14)	54
Equatorial Guinea					
Ethiopia	4,950	42	17	(12)	40
Gabon	3,320	11	51	N/A	38
Gambia					
Ghana	5,230	49	16	(10)	34
Guinea	2,540	30	32	(5)	38
Guinea-Bissau					
Kenya	7,380	31	20	(12)	49
Lesotho	330	21	28	(13)	52

Country					
Liberia					
Libya					
Madagascar	1,880	41	16	(11)	43
Malawi	1,080	37	18	N/A	44
Mali	1,940	49	12	(5)	39
Mauritania	900	38	21	N/A	41
Mauritius	1,600	13	33	(25)	54
Morocco	21,990	17	34	(18)	49
Mozambique	1,100	62	20	N/A	18
Niger	2,400	36	23	(9)	41
Nigeria	29,370	34	36	(18)	29
Rwanda	2,310	38	22	(15)	40
Sao Tome & Principe					
Senegal	4,980	22	29	(19)	49
Sierra Leone					·
Somalia	970	65	9	(5)	25
Sudan	11,240	33	15	(8)	52
Swaziland					
Tanzania	2,740	66	7	(4)	27
Togo	1,360	34	21	(8)	45
Tunisia	8,750	14	32	(16)	54
Uganda	3,950	72	7	(6)	20
Zaire	6,470	31	34	(7)	35
Zambia	4,000	14	43	(25)	43
Zimbabwe	5,650	11	43	(31)	46

Source: Ibid.

the candidate countries constitutes parameters that can be considered fixed for the purpose of investment decisions and again these are drawn out for each individual African country in Table IV.3. Actual recent performance in attracting foreign direct and portfolio investment is also an important indicator of aptitude to maintain a profitable business environment. This record as well is given in Table IV.4 for each individual African country. Other considerations are important, such as payments and exchange restrictions, labour laws, and the investment code, but often these are policy variables amenable to short-term adjustment in order to achieve given objectives.

Analysis of Tables IV.2 to IV.4 seems to indicate a list of no more than 14 African countries that could conceivably benefit substantially from the implementation of a full-blown debt-equity conversion programme. They are: Algeria, Cameroon, Côte d'Ivoire, Egypt, Ghana, Kenya, Libya, Mauritius, Morocco, Nigeria, Tunisia, Zaire, Zambia, Zimbabwe. This conclusion is premised on the assumption that investment through a debt-equity programme is more likely to be made in manufacturing and agricultural activities than in other subsectors, and a cut-off point of 10 per cent of GDP being of manufacturing-sector origin was used to demarcate efficient candidates for debt-equity conversion programmes from others. In addition, Zaire was included because of the size of its market. Furthermore, the basic-indicator profile was used to select candidate debtor countries with adequate domestic demand and/or adequate recent growth performance and macroeconomic management performance and/or adequate industrial characteristics, including urbanization. Of the short list of 14 countries, at least two were ruled out as efficient candidates for debt-equity conversion programmes, because their debt trades at nearly 100 cents on the dollar. These are Mauritius and Zimbabwe. Of the remaining 12, at least 4 have had an adverse or at least uncertain recent record in attracting foreign direct or portfolio investments, either because of socialist persuasions or poor macroeconomic performance. According to this accounting, 8 countries are left which offer sufficiently significant scope for a full-blown debt-equity conversion programme to be considered as capable of profitable implementation, with an adequate guarantee of success. They are: Côte d'Ivoire, Egypt, Ghana, Kenya, Morocco, Nigeria, Tunisia, and Zaire. Their total debt which creditors would consider offering on the market for debt-equity conversion if the terms were right amounts to $34.8 bn, or about 60 per cent of the total eligible or 27 per cent of the total commercial debt. This $34.8 bn is to be considered an upper limit, conditional on the assumptions that the debt-conversion mechanism operates efficiently, without any adverse side-effects, without restrictions and with adequate incentives to would-be investors. All these conditions are unlikely to be fully satisfied in reality, so that the scope is even less than the given figure indicates.

We must next consider the scope for debt buy-back on the demand side. Here again, the main factor is the creditors' perception both about the likelihood of African debtors having or building up excess reserves from which the resources would come to buy back the debt, and about the evolution in the availability of these reserves. Typically, if the perception is that, over an appropriate time-horizon, an excess reserves position is likely to be generated and maintained, creditors would be poised between two reactions: to insist on the servicing of the debt while holding on to the debt instruments (which has the effect of increasing the secondary market price), or to act decisively on converting the instruments into cash by selling at the market discount. The determining factor as to which of the two reactions will prevail is the creditor's assessment of the persistence or transitoriness of the excess reserves situation. If, overall, the excess reserves situation is seen as purely transitory and unlikely to remain sustainable over the medium term, the creditor is likely to want to sell, lest further deterioration of the debtor's economy lead to a cessation of servicing. However, this is not a clearcut two-outcome decision. At any given price, there will be a number of smaller bank paper-holders who will be ready to sell, while the larger creditors hold on. However, if the price is more attractive, a few of the larger creditors may come on to the market. These factors make for a relatively smoother demand schedule for buy-back than for debt-equity swaps.

Given the recent evolution of the reserves situations of most

Table IV.4 Foreign direct and portfolio investments in African countries (US$m.)

Country	1981	1982	1983	1984	1985	1986	1987	1988
Algeria	13	−57	N/A	1	N/A	5	4	15
Angola	2.1							−
Benin								
Botswana		21.1	23.8	62.2	53.6	70.4	113.6	39.9
Burkina Faso		2.8	2.4	1.7	−0.1	4.4		
Burundi	N/A	N/A	N/A	N/A	0.5	1.5	1.4	1.2
Cameroon	135.8	107.1	208.6	7.6	305.7	3.3	0.4	
Central African Rep.	5.8	8.8	4.0	4.9	2.4	6.9	9.3	
Chad		−0.1	−0.1	9.2	53.4	27.8	0.2	−12.6
Congo		35.3	56.1	34.9	12.7	22.4	43.4	9.1
Côte d'Ivoire		46.3	37.8	20.1	27.9	70.4	79.5	22.2
Egypt		285	477	714	1,195	1,211	931	1,178
Equatorial Guinea	N/A	N/A	N/A	N/A	N/A	N/A	−	−
Ethiopia	−	−	−	−		−	−	−
Gabon	N/A	127	106.1	4.8	11.1	103.7	82.2	121.4
Gambia		N/A	N/A	N/A	N/A	N/A	1.5	1.2
Ghana		16.3	2.4	2.0	5.6	4.3	4.7	5.0
Guinea								
Guinea-Bissau	−	−	−	−	−	−	−	−
Kenya		3.4	9.2	3.9	12.7	27.8	45.0	−19.4
Lesotho	4.8	3.0	4.8	2.3	4.8	2.1	5.7	21.0
Liberia	N/A	34.8	54.1	43.0	−9.8	−9.9	N/A	N/A

	-1,190	-654	-425	30	174	-244	-3,189	-179
Libya	-1,190							-179
Madagascar								
Malawi	3.0	3.3	3.0	1.0	0.9	1.3	4.3	0.8
Mali		1.5	3.1	4.1	2.9	-8.4	-6.0	-1.3
Mauritania	12.4	15.0	1.4	8.5	7.0	3.1	1.4	1.0
Mauritius		1.8	1.6	4.9	8.0	7.4	17.1	23.6
Morocco		80	46	47	20	-1	60	85
Mozambique								
Niger		24.9	2.2	3.9	-9.2	N/A	N/A	N/A
Nigeria		433	344	200	478	167	603	377
Rwanda		20.7	11.1	15.1	14.6	17.6	17.5	21.0
Sao Tome & Principe								
Senegal	18.9	10.7	-34.9	28.9	-18.3	-1.7	4.1	N/A
Sierra Leone	7.5	4.7	1.7	5.9	-31.0	-140.3	39.4	-23.1
Somalia		-0.8	-8.2	-14.9	-0.7	N/A	N/A	N/A
Sudan				9.1	-3.0			
Swaziland	N/A	-12.1	-6.2	2.5	15.3	25.3	38.9	47.4
Tanzania	N/A	N/A	N/A	N/A	N/A	N/A	N/A	N/A
Togo		15.9	1.3	-10.1	17.0	3.9	99	64
Tunisia		402	224	206	144	95	99	N/A
Uganda	N/A	N/A	N/A	N/A	N/A	N/A	N/A	N/A
Zaire	N/A	N/A	N/A	N/A	N/A	N/A	N/A	N/A
Zambia	-38	39	26	17	52	N/A	N/A	N/A
Zimbabwe	-26.4	-46.0	-44.8	-0.3	12.0	8.8	-29.6	N/A

Source: IMF, *Balance of Payments Statistics Yearbook*, 1990. Washington, DC.

African countries, it seems unlikely that holders of African debt paper are in any substantial number on the sidelines waiting to offer their paper for sale at a discount on the secondary market. They simply do not expect the African debtors to be able to generate the funds to buy back the debt, even if the discount is reasonable. In fact, this assessment was borne out by the interviews we carried out with investment and merchant bankers in early 1991 in the context of this study. A senior executive of one Britain's largest banks, with significant presence in most anglophone African countries, even asked ironically: 'And even if the banks were ready to take some loss on these loans and agreed to sell at a discount: where will the debtors get the money to buy them back?'. Furthermore, a quick glance down Table II.1 shows that, of the few countries with debt trade in the 30 to 50 per cent price range where significant deals are conceivable, only 4 out of the 21 listed had experienced even occasional deals. However, this should not marginalize the fact that a few of the financially stronger countries have, indeed, managed to buy back substantial portions of their debt on the secondary market at significant discounts. This has been the case notably for a couple of oil-exporting countries, and a couple of North African countries. At the time of writing, Nigeria is reported to be planning to reduce its debt by 60 per cent, a significant part through buy-back operations agreed in a March 1991 debt-restructuring exercise with the London Club of creditors.

The supply side:
the nature of counterpart assets to be ceded

The supply side of the debt-conversion transaction derives from the quantity and nature of counterpart assets which the African debtor country cedes in exchange for the debt paper. In the case of conversions through the debt-equity swap mechanism, these assets consist of equity participations in existing private enterprises, of portfolio investment in or takeover of newly privatised enterprises from which the government is disengaging within its privatization programme, and of equity holdings in new ventures launched jointly with local entrepreneurs or, where the investment code allows, with full foreign ownership. Where conversions take place through self-financed buy-backs, the assets ceded are cash flowing from balance-of-payments surpluses, and the scope for conversion then hinges entirely on the prospects for the generation of such surpluses.

A first assessment of the scope for debt-equity conversion from the supply-side perspective can be made from analysis of Tables IV.3 and IV.4. Table IV.3 gives the distribution of gross domestic production for each African country among the categories of agriculture, industry, and services, with the second of these subdivided between manufacturing and other. There is one subsector in the services sector of African countries that carries significant potential to attract interest among investors for debt conversion to acquire the funds for investment. This is the tourism sector. As the experience of Nigeria in debt-equity conversion (reviewed in Chapter 3) makes clear, this avenue provides a privileged method of converting a significant portion of the debt. The agricultural sector also provides significant investment prospects, with a potentially high rate of return and even of capital gain. However, the commitment by the prospective foreign investor needs to be for the longer term. Here, one needs to distinguish between takeovers of existing agricultural projects, the launching of totally new projects and investments in large estates producing export crops as opposed to medium-scale agricultural projects aiming mainly at the domestic market or as suppliers to agro-industries. In the case of takeovers and medium-scale agricultural projects, the commitment of investors need not be excessively long and pay-back periods may be short enough to generate considerable interest even among investors who do not already have a strong presence in the debtor country. Investment through conversion in large-scale plantations is likely to be limited to entrepreneurs who already have a strong presence in the debtor country.

The mining sector also provides good opportunities for foreign investment and has considerable potential to stimulate investor interest through debt-equity conversion. The oil sector is no doubt highly controlled, and foreign acquisition of equity in the industry is closely monitored and is unlikely to benefit from the additional incentives normally available under debt-equity conversion. However, oil-related industry, the petrochemicals sector and other activities linked to the oil sector, are, to some extent, eligible. Similarly, while the start of totally new ventures in the non-oil mining sector would require the same long-term commitment as totally new large-scale agricultural enterprises, and thus would probably be limited to investors already having a significant presence in the debtor country, these constraints do not apply to takeovers. Buying into existing mining enterprises while benefiting from the additional incentives of a debt-equity conversion thus also presents another major avenue for foreign investor interest in debt-equity swaps.

Examination of Table IV.4 indicates, however, that inward investment has not been on the uptrend in African countries in recent years and, furthermore, in the period 1986–8, no less than six countries have experienced at least one year of divestment. But these trends do not necessarily indicate a lack of investment opportunities in African countries with rates of return high enough to cover the investment costs of foreign investors, especially when the additional benefits of debt conversion are added. These trends more probably reflect the past distortions in prices, the structural deficiencies and disequilibria that not long ago characterized the majority of African countries. After several years of structural adjustment, of policy reform measures and the correction of disequilibria, the indications are that the stage is set for a revival of direct foreign investment, and the debt-equity conversion mechanism can be exploited fully to make the best possible use of this new setting. But the scope for debt conversion would, according to this line of argument, vary depending on how far each country had progressed in redressing its economy and making it responsive to private-sector activity.

Next, what is the scope for debt-equity conversion for investment in the industrial, and especially the manufacturing, sector? We have already pointed out that the industrial sector in most African countries is rather small and, as Table IV.3 shows, only about half of those with figures available have a manufacturing subsector which contributes at least 10 per cent of GDP to total activity. In our analysis of the demand side, it was brought out that, from the perception of the creditors, probably no more than 8 countries would be considered good prospects for the implementation of a full-blown debt-equity conversion programme, taking into account the requirements of foreign investment in manufacturing and agricultural activities. Now, from the supply-side perspective, it may be argued that the past record of attracting foreign investment need have no such restrictive impact on future prospects of doing so, if the proper policies, by way of revision of the investment code, designing of an appropriate privatization programme, and review of payments arrangements, are implemented. Already, however, the majority of African countries have been implementing privatization programmes for several years, but the record with regard to attraction of additional foreign investment has not been particularly encouraging. The problems may very well be the exiguity of domestic markets, the persistent barriers to freer intra-subregional and intra-regional trade, and the low quality-competitiveness of the African labour force and of products to capture the international market. In conclusion, based on the situation prevailing at present and which is likely to prevail in the short term, the scope for debt-equity conversion, even from the supply side, is quite narrow.

Finally, we turn to the scope for debt buy-back from the supply-side perspective. The determining variable here is the capacity of individual African countries to generate excess reserves, even of a relatively transitory nature, in order to buy back the debt at a substantial discount. Table IV. 5 presents the recent performance of individual African countries on the current accounts of their balances of payments. For the period 1981–8, no more than 12 countries in all were able to generate a surplus on their current accounts for as little as *two* years out of the eight covered. Of these, at least two countries would have their external debt valued at nearly 100 per cent on the secondary market, if they were quoted. Another three have very little external debt for any formal debt buy-back programme to be organized, other than on an ad hoc basis. Only Algeria, Morocco

Table IV.5 External current accounts performances of African countries (US$m.)

Country	1981	1982	1983	1984	1985	1986	1987	1988
Algeria	90	−183	−85	74	1,015	−2,230	141	−2,040
Angola								
Benin	−93	−377	−135	−57	5	−65	−74	−83
Botswana	−145	−82	−70	81	111	663	188	402
Burkina Faso		−92	−60	−3	−69	−118	−45	−59
Burundi					−42	−38	−96	−71
Cameroon	−482	−386	−412	−169	−561	−551	−893	
Central African Rep.	−4	−43	−29	−33	−49	−86	−75	
Chad		18	38	9	−87	−59	−25	25
Congo	−331	−401	−210	−161	−601			
Côte d'Ivoire		−1,016	−929	−73	68	−298	−949	−1,100
Egypt		−1,852	−330	−1,988	−12,166	−1,812	−245	−1,190
Equatorial Guinea							−24	−16
Ethiopia	−250	−195	−170	−130	106	−327	−217	−228
Gabon		309	72	113	−162	−1,058	−449	−616
Gambia		−22	−33	8	7	4	6	26
Ghana		−109	−174	−39	−134	−43	−97	−66
Guinea								
Guinea-Bissau		−35	−29	−36	−45	−20	−13	−29
Kenya		−302	−45	−123	−110	−37	−494	−454
Lesotho	−49	−38	−10	1	−17	−17	−12	−66
Liberia	75	2	−104	−2	56	15	−118	−66

Libya	−3,963	−1,560	−1,643	−1,456	−1,906	−156	−1,045	−1,823
Madagascar	−147	−299	−247	−193	−184	−141	−140	−149
Malawi		−118	−139	−49	−125	−90	−55	−53
Mali	−147	−115	−113	−117	−132	−173	−101	−92
Mauritania		−277	−213	−111	−116	−194	−147	−96
Mauritius		−43	−23	−55	−29	95	63	−63
Morocco		−1,878	−891	−989	−1891	−212	175	467
Mozambique								
Niger		−233	−62	1	−64	25	−90	−83
Nigeria		−7,285	−4,354	115	2,566	366	−69	−194
Rwanda		−87	−49	−42	−64	−69	−134	−119
Sao Tome & Principe		−25	−9	−11	−16	−19	−13	−11
Senegal	−462	−267	−306	−274	−273	−268	−257	−267
Sierra Leone	−132	−170	−18	−23	4	141	−30	−3
Somalia		−177	−142	−139	−103	−126	−114	−98
Sudan		−249	−219	25	155	−17	−232	−358
Swaziland		−112	−112	−84	−47	3	65	42
Tanzania		−524	−305	−359	−375	−321	−265	−376
Togo		−87	−43	26	−27	−56	−117	−57
Tunisia		−667	−578	−770	−587	−618	−60	213
Uganda	32	−70	−72	−103	5	−3.8	−131	−199
Zaire		−591	−349	−324	−289	−400	−654	−762
Zambia	−742	−566	−271	−153	−398	−299	−141	−196
Zimbabwe	−636	−709	−460	−100	−76	7	48	

Source: Ibid.

and Nigeria present characteristics which *a priori* would support the consideration of a formal programme of buy-back on a significant scale: they have, over the period considered, generated surpluses on their current accounts, their external debt is substantial, the offer of paper has considerable potential, and the discount is right – not so high as to hinder the offer of paper, not so low as to discourage the debtor.

However, this assessment of the scope for buy-back is somewhat restrictive. The excess reserves need not necessarily come from current account surpluses, but could also come from the capital account, including savings from foreign-exchange outflows from debt rescheduling and lowered debt service from debt conversion by means other than buy-back. This consideration opens up the possibility that, corrected for this factor, a somewhat larger number of countries than enumerated above could generate excess reserves for buy-backs. These would potentially include Cameroon, Côte d'Ivoire, Egypt, Gabon, maybe Madagascar, possibly Tanzania, Tunisia and also possibly Zaire among countries that could consider a significant-sized buy-back programme. Some of these countries are reported to be already undertaking just that, including Egypt. Of the first list, all three – Nigeria, Morocco and Algeria – have signed agreements to undertake buy-back operations.

With respect to the second list of countries, the operational consideration remains, if the excess reserves are not actual but only potential after adjusting for interest-service payments subsequent to other debt conversions, of how the buy-back will be financed in the first place. Two possibilities arise: bilateral aid from industrial-country partners specifically earmarked for debt buy-back, or resort to some type of multilateral facility, such as is considered in detail in Chapter 6.

5

The Cost-Benefit
Calculus and the Limits
to Debt Conversion

It should not be assumed as axiomatically true that debt reduction, by means of one or several of the conversion mechanisms considered here, is of unqualified benefit to the debtor country. The calculation of the benefits and costs to the economy of the debtor country of a debt-reduction programme through conversion is finely balanced, and has to take account of a few precisely quantifiable and many unquantifiable factors. The same type of calculus from the point of view of the creditor is even more indecisive. Therefore, any transactor, whether debtor or creditor, who decides to participate in a debt-conversion programme, has to analyse the complex interrelationships among the present level of external indebtedness, the prospects for generating budgetary and balance-of-payment surpluses before debt servicing in the debtor country, the level and dynamic of total investment in the country, the secondary effects of debt conversion on the secondary-market price of the remaining debt, and other economic, accounting and regulatory variables. In addition, the debtor country must keep in perspective the impact of debt conversion on its social, economic and political realities, while the creditor must weigh the effect of conversion on its after-tax profits, its balance sheet, and finally the market price of its shares if the creditor is a bank or a company.

In this chapter analysis of the principal benefits and drawbacks from debt reduction is confined to two conversion mechanisms: the debt-equity swap and the self-financed buy-back. The cost-benefit analysis for other types of conversion is done in the next chapter, along with discussion of important aspects of other conversion mechanisms. The list of the principal benefits and drawbacks from debt-equity conversion, investigated first from the debtor country's point of view, is longer than that for debt buy-back operations. We shall first limit ourselves to discussion of the benefits and drawbacks from the debtor's point of view, distinguishing between debt-equity and debt buy-back operations, before summarizing the same kind of analysis from the point of view of the creditor. From the outset we point out that this cost-benefit calculus must be weighed against a similar calculus derived from other conversion mechanisms and, above all, from the possibility of outright debt relief through non-market-based mechanisms. Discussion of these other mechanisms belongs in the next chapter.

The benefits

The principal benefits of debt-equity conversion may be analysed under seven items identified in the following list:

- reduction of debt and debt service,
- encouragement of foreign capital flows,
- spur to economic growth,
- encouragement of the repatriation of flight capital,
- risk reduction by replacing debt with equity,
- support of privatization programmes,
- boost to the transfer of technology.

The principal benefits, still from the point of view of the debtor country, deriving from debt buy-back operations, fall into a more restricted list of three items, as follows:

- reduction of debt service,
- enhancement of creditworthiness and access to capital market,
- spur to economic growth.

The rest of this section discusses each of these items in detail, giving empirical findings and evidence where available.

The direct benefit flowing from a successful debt-equity conversion programme is the reduction of the debt stock and of the debt-service obligations. The measurement of the extent of reduction of the debt stock is more complex than might appear at first sight. Even abstracting from the counterpart domestic assets that are ceded in the swap, the net amount of foreign exchange saved by the debtor is equal to neither the full amount of the debt swapped nor the discount multiplied by the amount of debt swapped. Various items in the structure of the fees payable to intermediaries have to be settled in foreign currency, and these have to be deducted from the 'first order' reduction in the stock. Moreover, when we include the local currency costs and receipts in the accounting, the net saving from a debt-equity conversion may amount to a fraction of between one-half and two-thirds of the amount of the nominal discount on the debt. This is because, to the various fees that have to be paid to intermediaries less the commissions charged by the Central Bank to process transactions, has to be added the exchange-rate subsidy which, in almost all cases, is granted to investors through debt-equity conversions.

As an example, consider the debt equity transaction detailed in Chapter 2, where $30 m. face-value of eligible debt is converted at a discount of 52 per cent. If we assume that there is no additionality in the investment – that is, the debt-equity swap replaces investment that would have been made anyway – the nominal 'immediate' foreign-exchange saving is $15.6 m. However, with an exchange-rate subsidy which sets the rate at 14.7 units of local currency to the dollar instead of 8 units, the foreign-exchange value of the subsidy, calculated at the subsidized rate, amounts to $7.02 m. The commissions encashed by the Central Bank less the fees paid to intermediaries may amount to about $1.17 m. (The conditions relating to this discussion are those elaborated in Chapter 2.) In sum, the actual saving is the discount captured by the country on a $30 m. debt-equity conversion and amounts to only $9.75 m. in the example, rather than the $15.6 m. that the simple application of the discount factor would indicate. That is equivalent to slightly over 60 per cent of the discount amount.

As regards the interest servicing of the debt, while payments are reduced to the full extent of the interest rate applied to the full amount of debt converted ($30 m. in the example), account has to be taken of the possibility that, when the equity investment generates sufficiently large profits and the delay on repatriation of profits is passed, dividends payments abroad will increase, and this tends to moderate the gain. In addition to drawbacks from debt-equity conversion by way of surrendering control of the economy to foreigners and other considerations which we shall investigate later in this chapter, it is pointed out that there are instances where, in the microeconomic financial management literature, the ultimate cost of equity finance is higher than that of debt. However, the argument fails to take account, within a macroeconomic setting, of 'second-order' benefits from debt-equity transactions, such as employment creation, increased tax revenues, greater access to export markets and long-term growth. This brings us to consideration of the indirect benefits of debt-equity conversion which constitute a longer list.

The most important of the secondary benefits of debt-equity conversion is its impact on the encouragement of foreign capital inflows. Theoretically, and according to evidence obtained from surveys, this is a straightforward and unequivocal consequence of the calculations of transnational corporations that they would be inclined to invest more if the cost of their funds were reduced. Given the pronounced decline that African countries have, on average, experienced in direct foreign investment, even from already very low levels, there is great attraction for them in the concept of utilizing debt-equity conversion programmes to attract new foreign capital inflows, even if the debt-reduction prospects may not be the primary aim. There are, however, two major problems for Africa. Firstly, as we saw in Chapter 2, the investment avenues for significant success to be achieved in attracting additional direct foreign investment in the majority of African countries just do not exist. Secondly, even in those few countries where the avenues are considerable, the issue of the 'additionality' of the investment is an important one. In essence, the 'additionality' problem questions whether the incentives given to the investor through a debt-equity transaction cause him genuinely to go into ventures which he would not have gone into otherwise and bring in capital which he would not otherwise have brought in. There has been much debate about this 'additionality' issue and the question is still unresolved.

From an empirical viewpoint, and as far as Africa is concerned, the evidence that exists on debt-equity conversion experiences in Zambia and Nigeria indicates that a moderate degree of 'additionality' is present in the foreign investments that have been undertaken under the programmes. The Latin American experience seems to be mixed. Chile, Argentina and Mexico appear to have had positive experiences of 'additionality' in foreign investment after the institution of their debt-equity conversion programmes, while Brazil was certain that it had good evidence that its programme was causing investors who would have brought in capital anyway to come in at a lower effective cost, and so at a loss to the country. In fact, this evidence was the major factor which caused Brazil to suspend its programme in

1987. As regards the Asian experience, one study[1] of the Philippine debt-equity conversion programme estimated that direct foreign investment in the Philippines under the debt-equity conversion programme had an 'additionality' effect totalling US$640 m. for the years 1986, 1987 and 1988. This compared to total investment for those three years of $1,331 m. Moreover, the 'additionality' factor gathered momentum over time. In 1986, the 'additional' investment amounted to $14 m. out of $140 m. in total; in 1987 it amounted to US$166 m. out of $205 m. in total, and in 1988 to $460 m. out of $986 m. in total.

The lesson to be borne in mind is that, for relatively diversified African economies where a full-fledged debt-equity programme may be cost-effective relative to the considerations spelt out in Chapter 4, there may be significant benefits in debt-equity swaps by way of catalyzing 'additional' foreign investment. For a few other African countries, ad hoc debt-equity swap transactions still have scope for generating incremental foreign investment that might not otherwise have been forthcoming. In the majority of cases, however, African countries should be wary of counting too much on debt-equity transactions acting as a significant catalyst for additional foreign investment. Rather, they may replace investment that would have been made anyway, and thereby involve the debtor country in unwarranted costs by way of subsidies.

A successful debt-equity conversion programme may also become a significant stimulant to growth. There are two channels through which this effect would operate. Firstly, by significantly reducing foreign debt-service obligations, a successful debt-equity conversion leaves a larger share of national income for domestic absorption, part of which one would normally expect to be channelled into investment. In turn, this investment is growth-stimulating. This effect is borne out by empirical investigations of the 'debt overhang' issue, which was discussed in Chapter 1. It was argued there that a 'debt overhang' situation

[1]Norman G. Dytimquin, *The Economics of Debt-Equity Swaps: An Empirical Investigation of the Macroeconomic Impact and Critical Analysis of the Effectiveness of the Philippine Debt-Equity Conversion Programme in External Debt Management*. The Hague: Institute of Social Studies, January 1990.

develops when the present value of expected future ability to pay is less than the value of the debt contracted. In such a case, full debt servicing resembles a distortionary tax and has the effect of encouraging consumption, since households feel that saving and growth will only go towards repaying creditors. Reducing the stock of debt then works in the interests of both debtors and creditors and is growth-stimulating. At the same time, that part of increased absorption which goes into consumption brings about a one-time increase in income through the multiplier effect.

Secondly, in so far as debt-equity conversion attracts additional foreign investment, opens up foreign markets and infuses new technology transfer, it is also growth-stimulating. While this argument is unassailable theoretically, the empirical evidence is mixed. A recent article by Ulrich Lächler and Peter Nunnenkamp[2] reported the results of their econometric investigations, which took explicit account of moral hazard problems, to test the claim that a capital-recipient developing country would be better-off with a lower debt-equity ratio. In other words, their model tested whether a capital-recipient country would achieve a higher saving rate, investment rate and growth rate with a strong debt-equity conversion programme in place. The results of their investigations showed that the capital transfer negotiations between foreign creditors and the managing authorities of a developing country revealed 'non-cooperative equilibrium' characteristics. In such situations, the choice between equity and debt-financed inflows has been shown to exhibit a 'risk-return' trade-off between income stability and expected growth. In other words, with a higher proportion of equity-financed inflows, the variability of residual income generated and retained in the developing economy declines, but the domestic savings incentives, and hence the growth prospects of that economy, are also not much improved.

One main reason for this lack of improvement in the growth rate is that equity finance tends partly to replace domestic

[2]Ulrich Lächler and Peter Nunnenkamp, 'The effects of debt versus inflows on savings and growth in developing economies'. Kiel Institute of World Economics. *Weltwirtschaftliches Archiv,* Vol. 123, No 4, 1987.

investment and also to reduce the savings rate. The general result is that, while debt-financed capital inflows exert a relatively stronger positive influence on domestic savings and growth, they also generate variability in income and consumption. Equity-financed transfers, by contrast, do reduce the variability in income and consumption, but have very little positive effect on savings and growth.

The fourth source of benefits from debt-equity conversion programmes is their potential for encouraging the repatriation of capital. The more fortunate nationals of many capital-short countries have for a long time held their capital abroad, in very rare cases (as in Venezuela not long ago) legally, in all other cases illegally. The pernicious policy of maintaining overvalued exchange rates for long periods has encouraged this economically perverse habit. A few, especially Latin American, countries have devised debt-conversion programmes specially tailored to attract such flight capital, and have experienced considerable success. Chile's highly successful Chapter 18 programme (briefly reviewed in Chapter 3) is a case in point. Other countries started off debarring residents or nationals resident abroad from participating in their debt-equity conversion programmes in order to avoid any possible public uproar that past perpetrators of economic crimes should be rewarded at the expense of domestic investors and the public at large. But some later felt that they were missing out on some alluring means of bringing in much-needed capital, and they therefore relaxed the regulations. It must, however, be borne in mind that the principal countries that have manifestly encouraged the repatriation of flight capital through debt-equity conversion are the larger countries with quite diversified economies, where the capital-flight problem has long been particularly visible to the point of ostentation. The amount that could be tapped was thus very large.

There are few serious studies of capital flight in African countries. A recent study[3] estimates the cumulative net private

[3]P.H. Kevin Chang and Robert E. Cumby, 'Capital Flight in Sub-Saharan African Countries'. Paper presented at the World Bank Symposium on African External Finance in the 1990s. Washington, DC: World Bank, September 1990.

capital outflows from 36 sub-Saharan African countries between 1976 and 1987 as being in the range of 10 to 15 per cent of their annual per capita income, with by far the larger part of this amount attributable to only 9 countries. Outflows from Nigeria are estimated to have constituted nearly half of this total, while Sudan also accounted for a significant proportion of nearly 20 per cent. In view of these estimates, it would seem inadvisable for most African countries to envisage tailoring any debt-equity conversion programme they may want to instal specifically to attract flight capital. This caution is reinforced by the consideration that giving such incentives to former operators in illegal transactions is politically sensitive. At the same time, however, sufficiently restrictive constraints can be placed on nationals who bring in flight capital to limit their profiting from the additional incentives of a debt-equity swap, in such a way as to ensure both that the recipient country benefits and that those who object that crime is being rewarded are appeased.

The fifth source of benefits from debt-equity conversion, namely, the fact that it reduces risk by replacing debt with equity, has to some extent already been analysed when we discussed its growth-stimulating effect with the help of a principal-agent model. The results of the empirical investigation reported above implied that the implementation of a debt-equity programme would reduce the capital-recipient country's variability in income and consumption (because dividends would be paid only if sufficient profits are generated, while interest obligations are fixed and mandatory), while the maintenance of the existing debt equity structure leaves the country vulnerable to fluctuations in residual income after fixed interest and amortization payments are made. On the other hand, however, there exists the possibility that equity obligations may in the long run prove more expensive than debt obligations, because future dividend payments may be substantial and capital repatriation may even occur. But this counter-argument assumes that the project to which the proceeds of the debt-equity swap go proves to be highly profitable, in which case the larger part of the profits accrue to the creditor/investor. The balance of the two arguments then rests upon whether the project would have been undertaken even in the absence of the debt-equity conversion programme. In the case of Africa, it is fairly safe to say that the risk-reducing aspect of debt-equity conversion is positive, because the scarcity of capital (and possibly even of entrepreneurship and knowhow) is so high that many ventures with potentially high returns are not embarked upon because of the dearth of foreign direct investment.

The fact that debt-equity conversion programmes can stimulate the government's privatization policy in the African countries where state-run enterprises, mostly loss-making, have a significant presence, has caused these countries to enter actively into several ad hoc debt-equity transactions even without consideration of whether they may want to have a full-fledged conversion programme or not. One of the more direct ways by which a privatization policy finds strong support in a debt-equity conversion programme is by the state enterprise which is to be privatized trading in its shares in exchange for its own foreign debt. This process has the additional advantage of short-circuiting a number of intermediaries and also, from the debtor country's point of view, of dominating the inflationary money-creation problem inherent in buying the debt in exchange for local currency. In fact, the explicit rationale of the Chilean programme was to facilitate the return to the private sector of enterprises that had been either set up and run by the government or taken over and subsidized by it. The marked presence of the government in many sectors of activity in African countries would make this consideration a strong one to weigh in for those countries which could envisage instituting either ad hoc or full-scale conversion programmes. It must be cautioned, however, that there are simultaneously many strategic and security reasons, as well as political considerations, why certain state enterprises have to remain – and in certain cases, indeed, have remained – off limits to privatization by debt-equity. There are also economic reasons, including the impact on employment and the possible displacement of other investment, which we shall investigate when we consider the drawbacks from debt-equity conversion.

The final source of benefits from debt-equity conversion

programmes to be considered here is the possibility of the boost they can give to the transfer of technology to the debtor country. Indeed, most debt-equity conversion plans, including the Nigerian one, explicitly list the potential for transfer of technology as a main determinant for the eligibility of a project for debt-equity conversion. However, while it is true that conversion allows more channels to monitor and enhance effective transfer of technology than do normal foreign direct investment inflows, the practical monitoring of the effective transfer of technology remains elusive. Yet the allure is so intense that this factor is one not to be overlooked in decisions whether to implement debt-equity conversion programmes in a formal, full-scale manner, or not. And this is rightly so, for few triads carry more potential for the transformation of indebted developing economies and for the generation of sustained growth than the debt-reduction/capital inflow/technology-transfer process.

Next, we turn to the benefits flowing from debt buy-back operations. As pointed out above, these fall essentially into three main categories. The first, direct benefit is, as in the debt-equity conversion case, simply the reduction of debt and debt service. Again in this case, measurement of the benefit involves some, but not all, of the complications we found in the debt-equity conversion case. However, unlike debt-equity transactions, there are no future contingent dividend payments to be taken into account, so that, to that extent, the calculation of the benefit from debt reduction is simplified. But an added complication crops up because, under certain conditions, even imperfectly competitive ones, a significant-sized buy-back operation has the undesirable effect of increasing the price on the secondary market of the remaining debt, equivalently reducing the discount. Therefore, the amount of debt reduction has to be netted of the amount by which the remaining debt's secondary-market price is increased. The derivation of the calculations is explained for the purely theoretical, full-information, perfect-competition case, in the Appendix. The calculations for the more likely imperfect-competition case cannot be made precisely, but lie somewhere between the no-response case and the full-adjustment case. As for interest service on the debt, it is reduced by the full amount of the relevant interest rate applied to the full face-value of the buy-back.

In addition to the reduction in the debt stock and in debt service, buy-back operations have the effect of enhancing the creditworthiness of the implementing country, and of upgrading its access to capital markets. The enhancement of creditworthiness results from the manifest decline in future debt-servicing obligations brought about by the buy-back, coupled with the internalization of the discount which the country captures on the secondary market. In other words, the foreign-exchange earnings that are likely to be available in future years to service the remaining lower level of debt, are increased, and therefore their present value – which translates into the creditworthiness of the country – increases. As a result, it can be expected that the cost of funds to the debtor country is lowered, that the country could consequently move further along its investment schedule and therefore that more projects become lucrative. The precise amount of the benefit could be measured if the investment schedule of the firm is known, since the cost-of-funds effect can be precisely calculated. Very few countries, apart from Bolivia, have so far bought back a significant part of their debt, so that not much empirical evidence exists to support or invalidate the above theoretically sound conclusions. However, it is known that Bolivia did not reap much benefit from buy-back either by way of manifestly improved creditworthiness or enhanced access to international capital markets. But then Bolivia's case cannot be considered typical. The reported recent (late March 1991) plans of Nigeria to buy-back up to 60 per cent of its commercial debt would be an interesting case to follow up. *A priori*, it seems clear that buy-backs, at secondary-market prices of between 20 and 40 per cent, present an attractive means at least of reducing debt, even if the creditworthiness-improving argument is debatable. But even this half-pessimism does not need to be justified. The real question in buy-backs is where the funds to carry out the operations come from.

Finally, there is also the growth-stimulating effect of buy-backs. This effect operates through three channels, two of them making a positive contribution, the third one negative. Firstly, in so far as debt buy-backs reduce future debt-servicing obligations, they leave for absorption into the economy, either as consumption or as investment, a larger proportion of total production than would otherwise be available. If the larger part of this available output goes for higher consumption, there is a large one-shot increase in the level of activity, through the multiplier effect, and a smaller growth effect, resulting from increased investment. If the increased availability is used predominantly for investment, the growth effect is much more important, while the impact effect of the level of activity is muted. The second channel through which the growth effect works itself out is the increased inflow of foreign capital resulting from improved creditworthiness. If external debt management is sound and fresh foreign funds are channelled into projects with rates of return higher than the cost of funds (which has now been lowered), the additional output generated feeds into higher growth even after increased debt-service obligations are made. The reverse side of this transmission process is the third, negative channel, whereby the diversion of foreign-exchange resources that would otherwise have been used for investment or intermediate input imports is utilized to buy back debt. This diversion of resources has the effect of slightly setting back growth, except in cases where all of the resources would alternatively have gone into consumption. Nonetheless, on balance the three effects combined have the result of stimulating growth, since the face-value of the debt bought back is higher than the value of the resources spent.

The drawbacks

The actual practice of debt conversion in the relatively few countries that have implemented such programmes has confirmed that they can have serious drawbacks. In fact, the majority of implementing countries have had, at one point or another, seriously to modify their programmes to correct for adverse side-effects, or to institute auxiliary programmes to counter these side-effects, or to suspend the programmes outright for a period. A number of these drawbacks have been identified as being common to several or all of the implementing countries, but before listing them and proceeding to analyse their effects, it is important to repeat a theoretical argument about one drawback from conversion, namely the possibility that over the longer term equity may prove more expensive than debt as a financing method. This would be because, if the investment into which the equity funds go proves profitable, the present value of a perpetual future dividend outflow may become higher than the face-value of the debt. However, we found above that there are also second-order benefits to debt-equity conversion which this argument ignores. In the final analysis, the question whether the benefits from debt-equity conversion outweigh the drawbacks will depend on each individual case.

The principal drawbacks from debt-equity conversion arise from concerns about the following issues:

- the degree of 'additionality' in foreign investment
- the degree of tolerance of foreign penetration of the domestic economy
- the misallocation of resources brought about by distortions resulting from exchange-rate subsidies
- 'round-tripping'
- the side-effect of stoking inflationary pressures.

Measures can be taken to alleviate these problems, and they are discussed below.

The issue of the 'additionality' of foreign investment, already discussed at some length above from a positive angle, has a reverse side which entails costs to the debtor country when the negative effect predominates, namely, that new investment only replaces investment that would have been made anyway. In such situations, the financial inflow into the debtor country is less than would have occurred if the debt-equity programme had not been in place, and, in addition, adverse side-effects, such as distortions caused by exchange-rate subsidies, would not have resulted. On an empirical basis, it is a fact, as pointed out above, that a couple of countries – namely, Chile and the Philippines – have been able to attract sufficient additional foreign investment through debt-equity conversion programmes to make the experience highly beneficial overall. But the experience of other countries, such as Mexico, is not very happy on this count. As for African countries, while it may be argued that *normal* foreign direct investment is in general so low that any investment that occurs through debt-equity swap is 'additional' anyway, it is also evident that this general case applies to countries that would, on other counts, find it inadvisable to implement formal full-scale debt-equity swap programmes, so that the positive additionality argument becomes hollow. As for African countries that would otherwise find a formal debt-equity swap programme beneficial, the additionality of foreign investment is uncertain. Such is the case, for example, for Nigeria. In conclusion, the additionality factor, balancing the benefits and the drawbacks, does not have much positive impact to recommend it as an important consideration in the decision to implement a debt-equity programme.

The issue of foreign penetration of the domestic economy and of foreign control is an emotive and complex one. Foreign technology is sorely needed to exploit efficiently the resources – mining but also agricultural and potentially industrial – of the larger African countries. Pending the long-awaited integration of fragmented African markets, foreign investment also brings with it vastly increased market accessibility. However, because of the limited sources of the supply of foreign capital, the price and incentive structures – return to capital, foreign workers' salaries, wages, tax holidays – tend to be out of line with normal domestic practice. Furthermore, foreign companies' activities tend to be highly visible. Hence the 'economic rent' – above-normal profits or other incentives – which a country would logically be ready to pay to acquire these oligipolistically supplied benefits, is vociferously opposed by nationalists who marshal arguments of preferential treatment, sell-out and loss of control to foreigners. The real thrust of the argument is political. Economically, there are strong arguments in support of opening up the economy to foreign investment, with the usual considerations of balancing economic benefits against costs. But the citizenry's perceptions also constitute a variable in the decision-making process. Nevertheless, in recent years many African countries have become more receptive to foreign investment and the market-forces orientation it entails. As a consequence, the loss-of-control argument as a drawback from debt-equity conversion is becoming weaker.

The issue of the misallocation of resources resulting from distortions caused by subsidies paid to investors through debt/equity transactions is a serious one. In essence, the foreign investor is allowed to undertake investment expenditures – acquiring physical capital and good will, hiring labour and deriving dividends – at a lower cost than his domestic counterparts. This causes distortions that may discourage domestic investment, encourage excessive consumption by discouraging saving for investment and thereby cause serious ill effects to the macroeconomy. A couple of countries have tried to counter these adverse effects by allowing nationals who hold foreign exchange also to buy into external debt for debt-equity conversion. But then in countries that have strict exchange control, the regulatory question arises of how such foreign exchange can be legally acquired. The fact that not all activities are eligible for debt-equity conversion only partly resolves the distortionary-effect argument. But again, the same situation applies to all other investment codes that try to encourage foreign investment, although the distortions are less visible. The most that can be done is the 'second-best' solution of applying distortion-correcting measures as close as possible to the source of the perceived distortion. What the exact measures are will depend on the specifics of each case and of each type of distortion.

The problem of 'round-tripping' arises from the tempting possibility offered by the debt-conversion mechanism for operators in the external sector of a debtor country's economy to make additional easy profits by grafting their usual trade on to debt-conversion deals. Nationals involved in the export business and transnational corporations earning foreign exchange become easy victims of the temptation to withhold at least part of their foreign-exchange earnings and use them to buy back debt at a discount, cash in on the subsidy in local currency and, instead of investing the profits in eligible investments, finance further export trade to restart the whole process again. More perniciously, even nationals not generating foreign-exchange earnings by their trade are tempted to buy foreign exchange on the local parallel market in order to buy back debt at a deep discount, cash it in local currency and possibly restart the whole process again. The 'round-tripping' problem is one that has been of concern to several countries. At least two easy *solutions* suggest themselves to counter the problem, but they have their own adverse side-effects. Firstly, it is possible significantly to reduce the contamination area from 'round-tripping', by prohibiting nationals from participating in the debt-conversion programme. Mexico and a number of other countries have done just that. The adverse side-effect is that the debtor country must then rule out the possibility, even at a later date, of encouraging the repatriation of flight capital, since this would require allowing nationals to participate. Otherwise, it would have to revert to opening up the 'round-tripping' temptation. Furthermore, excluding nationals from participation only partly resolves the problem, because transnationals can always continue to do 'round-tripping'. The second possible solution is to tighten exchange and capital controls, but this can also have an adverse psychological impact on potential *bona fide* investors, and can reduce 'additionality'. Nigeria has been able to resolve the round-tripping problem relatively successfully by a combination of monitoring the sources of the funds with which the external debt is acquired and utilization of the local currency proceeds of debt conversion. Furthermore, as the gap between the parallel market exchange rate and the official exchange rate is closed, one avenue for round-tripping is also blocked.

Finally, the problem that debt-equity conversion programmes tend to increase the pace of inflationary pressures on the domestic economy is one that all countries implementing debt-conversion programmes have had to face. When it is the government that is retiring its own debt, the process by which inflationary pressure is created is evident. For, in that case, the buyer of the external debt does not syphon off from the domestic money supply funds to acquire foreign exchange to buy the debt, but rather obtains credit from the domestic banking system (in other words, creates an increase in credit to the government or what is commonly termed 'printing money') to pay in local currency. The increase in the money supply causes inflation. It may be possible to 'sterilize' the impact of the debt conversion by issuing local currency bonds, which has the effect of mopping up the additional money injected into the economy. However, this increases interest rates and has adverse effects of its own. Besides, most African countries do not yet have a capital market deep and sophisticated enough to absorb such a flotation of bonds easily.

Alternatively, the debtor government can alleviate the inflationary impact by earmarking part of its budget expenditures specifically to finance debt redemptions for equity, in effect reducing its other expenditures and, in the end, its deficit financing. However, since this is tantamount to bunching up several future years' debt-servicing obligations into one year, this course is politically impracticable. The more practical course, and the one followed by most countries that are currently implementing debt-equity conversion programmes, is to operate an annual quota system so that the quantum of debt-equity conversion allowed is in line with developments in the monetary sector. Even with such a system, at least one country, Mexico, has experienced problems which necessitated a suspension of the programme. But, when all is said and done, the inflation problem remains manageable.

With regard to debt buy-back, there are essentially two important drawbacks:

- the opportunity cost of the alternative use of resources
- the fact that the offer price on the secondary market tends to go up with each buy-back operation.

The first issue of the opportunity cost of the alternative use of resources is a complex one. At first sight, it does not seem to be a problem at all if the foreign exchange used to buy back the debt is in excess of what is required for essential uses. This conclusion follows from the fact that a substantial discount is available on the face-value of the debt, and therefore the present value of discounted future obligations, which are annulled by the buy-back, is significantly higher than the amount of foreign exchange spent to buy back the debt. Further analysis reveals, however, that this argument assumes that the rate by which future debt-servicing obligations are discounted is no higher than the rates of return obtainable from new investments that could alternatively have been undertaken with the excess foreign exchange. If rates of return on alternative projects are higher, future obligations need to be discounted by these higher rates and compared to the cost of the buy-back. If the cost of the buy-back is still lower, then the opportunity-cost problem does not arise. However, there are also other advantages to holding on to foreign-exchange reserves, which are not directly quantifiable, to balance against the reduction of future debt-service obligations, although these would also be in foreign exchange. On balance, however, when windfall increases in foreign-exchange revenues occur, buying back the external debt at a discount in the region of 50 per cent or more is likely to be quite beneficial.

The problem caused by the tendency for offer prices to rise on the secondary market with each buy-back operation can be tackled by a combination of astute market 'signals' and tight negotiations with creditors. This is the area where the 'game' aspect of the sovereign debt problem becomes most evident. The types of market 'signals' sent to creditors range from publicizing balance-of-payments and other macroeconomic forecasts which only implicitly, but very forcefully, take account of the government's priorities in managing its finances, to announcing an imminent suspension of debt servicing, including interest servicing. An example of the former type would be when a debtor government publicizes financing gaps derived from deliberately underestimated export earnings, and/or domestic output growth, as well as other macroeconomic aggregates. Such action does not constitute reprehensible misinformation, but the implicit deduction from actual export earnings of the foreign exchange the debtor government wishes to set aside to buy back its debt, combined with equivalent adjustments in domestic fiscal expenditures.

This practice has parallels on the creditors' side, such as when they hike the charges and commissions payable by debtors on trade credit when their perceived creditworthiness has suffered, even if accepted practices call for a lower interest rate and lower charges and commissions. This action also 'signals' deteriorating creditworthiness to the debtor in a forceful but implicit way. The bargaining component of the strategy is complex, but one rule that can be spelt out with certainty is that, if a buy-back of significant size is contemplated, it should *never* be done piecemeal; the whole package should be negotiated with the creditors under binding agreements to sell at a price not noticeably above the market prices prevailing prior to the announcement of the intention to buy back.

Benefits and drawbacks
from the creditor's perspective

Successful voluntary (market-based) debt conversion cannot take place to any significant degree without the existence of perceptible benefits for the creditors as well. Although, *a priori* there seem to be only costs involved for the creditors in debt conversion by way of the discounts at which they sell their debt, there are in fact significant benefits also. As before, we shall distinguish between debt-equity conversion and debt buy-back.

There are three important sources of benefit to the creditors from debt-equity conversion, in addition to several secondary sources. The main sources are:

- the subsidies on the exchange rate, tax holidays and other investment incentive packages, as well as the possibilities that future profits will exceed in present value terms the face-value of the debt;
- for banks, but also for suppliers of trade credits, the opportunity of portfolio enhancement; this involves asset diversification, and risk reduction. For banks, there is also the opportunity to upgrade the balance sheet by reducing the need

for provisioning against doubtful loans;
- the link between debt and trade; as the debt problems of developing countries are eased, their demand for imports rises, so that the opportunities for banks and trade-credit suppliers to increase their activity become broader.

The first source of benefits, namely the investment incentives package and future profits, has already been analysed at some length. It constitutes the main attraction for creditors to convert debt through equity-swaps. At times this attraction has been strong enough to make one authoritative researcher[4] complain that: 'In fact the banks have become increasingly aggressive in recent negotiations, unrestrained by any discipline of public policy. The banks pressed for extensive debt-equity swap programs and relending provisions for Brazil thus contributing markedly to Brazil's hyperinflation . . .'. On the other hand, however, as we have argued above, there are strong primary and significant secondary benefits from debt-equity conversion to the debtor countries as well, so that the mechanism provides considerable scope for the convergence of creditor and debtor interests.

Secondly, debt-equity conversion provides creditors with a very good opportunity for portfolio enhancement. Prior to negotiating a debt-equity swap operation, a creditor, be it a bank or a supplier of trade credit, is carrying among its assets debt instruments of impaired value. In the case of banks, provisioning against doubtful loans is also likely to have been made. A successful debt-equity conversion allows the creditor to change its asset composition so that, even if it assumes more risk both of a loss and of a profit, it diminishes the certainty of a proportional loss of more significant size in terms of expected value. In the case of banks, it also opens up the possibility of writing down loan-loss provisions, which has the effect of increasing their share value on the market.

The third source of benefit to the creditor relates to the link

---

[4]Jeffrey Sachs, *Efficient Debt Reduction*. op. cit.

between debt and trade. The main activity of most of the banks significantly engaged in arranging debt-equity transactions is trade financing, and they see the debt problem, even with its opportunities of bringing in income by arranging debt-equity deals, as a major hindrance. This is even more true for other suppliers of trade credit, who may be the exporters themselves. As debt-equity conversion reduces the pressures of the debt problem, debtor countries increase their imports. This restores the normal situation of trend growth in exports to these countries, and the bankers and exporters/trade-credit suppliers benefit.

As far as the benefits from debt buy-back are concerned, there seem to be only two main sources from the creditor's point of view:

• portfolio enhancement
• the link between debt and trade.

Since the creditor sells back the debt instrument it holds at a discount, and obtains in return only a reduced payment in the same currency in which it was originally supposed to be paid back, it seems at first sight to incur only a cost. However, prior to the buy-back, the creditor was holding a paper asset of impaired value. If the creditor is a bank, it may also have made provisioning against a doubtful loan, which is not yet tax-deductible. If the bank sells the debt, even at a discount, it not only enhances its portfolio by converting a paper asset of deteriorating value into cash, but also reduces the liabilities side of its balance sheet by writing off the loan-loss provision partly against actual loss and partly against tax credit. The extent of this benefit depends on the regulatory provisions in the creditor's country.

The second source of benefits of debt buy-back from the creditor's point of view is the link between debt and trade. Here, the same argument applies as we have just drawn with regard to debt-equity conversion. For the offers of debt instruments for buy-back operations come mainly from the same creditors as are engaged in debt-equity swap transactions, namely commercial banks and trade-credit suppliers/exporters. The drawbacks from both debt-equity swaps and debt buy-backs, as viewed by the primary creditors, are quite evident. Firstly, there is the discount which they have to assume when they surrender debt instruments at less than face-value. Secondly, in the case of debt-equity conversion, it involves the creditors in lines of business where they do not have a comparative advantage, and as such subjects them to the risk of loss. Thirdly, there are numerous regulatory constraints in creditor countries on equity participation by banks, on selling debt instruments at below face-value and claiming a loss for tax purposes, as well as on other accounting practices.

The limits to debt conversion in Africa

In addition to the limits on the scope for debt conversion in African countries arising from the above cost-benefit consideration and the analysis in Chapter 4, other operational factors draw additional limits. The following four deserve special attention:

 i. programme design: types of conversion, incentives, and bilateral or syndication procedures;
 ii. the activism of banks or agents in pushing the deals;
 iii. the cost-benefit calculus of the exchange of assets and political considerations regarding foreign control;
 iv in the case of buy-backs, the cost-benefit calculus of the alternative uses of funds.

With regard to programme design, whether the chosen debt-conversion mechanism is of the debt-equity type or debt buy-back (or even, conceivably, a debt-debt swap), it is always possible to add incentives or modify restrictions in order to make a programme more interesting. Among the incentives that a debtor government can work into the design of a programme are the following:

(a) the provision of a list of attractive projects eligible for debt-conversion deals;
(b) the reduction to a minimum of any pre-qualification require-ments for an auction system, if this method is used;
(c) permission to use the proceeds of debt conversion to buy into investment funds which hold equity in several eligible projects;
(d) simplification of conversion and investment approval procedures;
(e) flexibility in the timing of disbursement of local currency;
(f) enhancement of tax concessions or holidays and easing dividend-remittance constraints;
(g) institution of a liberal investment code; and
(h) a general commitment to a stable macroeconomic climate favouring foreign investment.

Policy measures help towards enlarging the scope for debt-equity conversion, but they cannot fundamentally modify the constraints spelled out in Chapter 4 on supply and demand. However, two other issues must not be lost sight of in discussing the scope for debt conversion. Firstly, while debt reduction is no doubt a primary goal of conversion, other important objectives include the possibility of catalyzing additional foreign invest-ment, of helping a privatization programme or of furthering another of the subsidiary goals spelled out in Chapter 1. Thus, even if the basic constraints cannot be changed, enhancing the scope by fine-tuning the incentives furthers the achievement of the other goals. Secondly, even for the majority of countries whose characteristics do not point to a viable debt-equity conversion programme on a significant scale, ad hoc debt-conversion deals can yield non-negligible benefits both by way of marginal reduction of the debt stock *and* by way of achieving one or more of the subsidiary goals. To the extent that fine-tuning the incentives succeeds in attracting creditor interest even in those countries, the scope for debt-equity conversion is enhanced.

Another consideration not to be lost sight of is the procedural mechanism for conversion. The debtor country may contact investment banks or accounting firms to design and manage the programme for it, or it may choose to institute an auction system within its Central Bank. When an agent such as an investment bank or an accounting firm is chosen to implement the programme, there arises the possibility of setting up a fund into which numerous small investors could buy and managed by the agent on their behalf, which would then invest in eligible projects. Zambia and Nigeria were presented with such proposals, but both declined because they felt doubtful about giving such powers to private companies.

A related consideration that arises, in line with this argument, is the activism of banks or agents in pushing the deals if a large-scale debt-equity, or for that matter debt buy-back, programme is instituted. As noted in Chapter 2, it is not uncommon for banks to trade assets on their own behalf, and also to carry a portfolio, giving clients an option to buy debt paper which would later be submitted for pre-qualification. To enhance the chances of a debt-conversion programme materializing into additional new investment, the debtor country needs to implement the procedural regulations analysed in Chapter 2 *and also* ensure that the investment banks are active in selling paper to potential investors. Adequate negotiations with banks familiar with the debtor country's affairs, and preferably with a presence in the country, are called for to enhance the scope for conversion.

Two final considerations relate to the cost-benefit calculus involved, first, in giving up national assets to foreign control in order to reduce debt, and, second, in utilizing scarce foreign exchange to buy back debt. With regard to the first, there is no denying the continuation, in many of the better-endowed African countries, of a negative attitude towards foreign investment. For one, the oil sector is highly controlled, and significant foreign investment is allowed only after elaborate political considerations. Other sensitive sectors that are considered vital for national security are also restricted. Although in recent years attitudes towards foreign investment have been changing, they still limit somewhat the scope for debt-equity conversion.

As for the cost-benefit calculus of utilizing scarce foreign-exchange resources to buy back debt, the issue is whether the present value of future *inevitable* debt service (that is, which cannot be postponed or avoided) on the amount of debt which is reduced, is greater than the foreign exchange which is used to buy back the debt. If it is, then buy-back is worthwhile. The catch in this simple solution is the rate of return by which future debt service should be discounted. The rate would be higher than the prevailing interest rate on the debt itself, because the marginal utility of the return of reserves to the debtor country is presumably higher than the rate of interest, since foreign capital is rationed to it. But at the same time, the absolute amount of future servicing payments that is discounted is higher than the amount of reserves paid up because the debt sells at a discount. In general, it can be estimated that, if the debt is traded in the 20 to 40 per cent range, and the current account surpluses are transitory, and at the same time no debt relief is likely in the short run, then buy-back is beneficial in terms of the cost-benefit calculus of the alternative use of reserves.

6

Concerted
Debt-Reduction
Schemes

The clear conclusion has emerged from the foregoing analysis
that, except for a few of the larger African countries with relatively diversified economies, the scope for the two most important market-based debt-reduction mechanisms (debt-equity
swaps and debt buy-back), each taken separately, significantly to
reduce the stock of outstanding debt is rather limited. There are,
of course, other market-based debt-conversion mechanisms,
such as debt-for-nature swaps, debt-for-development, bilateral
debt-for-commodity arrangements, and various versions of
bilateral debt-for-debt swaps, but these also remain of limited

applicability for reasons partly discussed in Chapter 1. However, *multilateral* arrangements based on debt-for-commodity conversion or the various versions of debt-for-debt swaps, and backed by the support of an international agency, *do* have significant potential for resolving the debt problem. Indeed, a leading analyst argues that this approach may be the only meaningful way of bringing about significant debt reduction.[1]

> The gap between the rhetoric of debt reduction and the harsh reality of debt negotiations for the debtor countries has never been greater. In the past two years, debt restructuring programs have done little to satisfy the financial needs of the debtor countries. . . . The failure . . . to make real headway with debt reduction is not an accident. Even when a reduction of the debt burden would be beneficial to the broad class of creditors and debtors alike, it is unlikely to emerge from the current structure of debt negotiations. Meaningful debt reduction requires an appropriate institutional setting to overcome important collective action problems. . . . Instead of 'voluntary' debt reduction, we need 'concerted' debt reduction.

A concerted debt-reduction scheme is a programme worked out by the debtor country in collaboration with the international financial institutions and other creditors with a view to restructuring and reducing its debt. Most important, it overcomes collective-action problems such as the equal-sharing clauses discussed earlier and 'free-rider' problems whereby a bank not participating in a debt-reduction transaction can benefit at the participants' cost. It also facilitates movement to the optimal point on the 'debt-relief Laffer curve' discussed in Chapter 1. The present chapter analyses such concerted approaches to debt reduction. It still keeps within the context of debt owed to commercial banks and to private suppliers, so that Paris Club initiatives such as the Toronto Plan are omitted. The schemes we investigate are the existing World Bank debt buy-back facility and menu-based, Brady-style concerted debt-reduction schemes such as a few countries have recently tried out. The chapter

---

[1]Jeffrey Sachs, *Efficient Debt Reduction*. op. cit., pp. 4–5.

concludes with an analysis of the benefits deriving from such schemes and the difficulties in implementing them. It also makes a tentative assessment of the implementation of the menu-based concerted programmes in two countries that have implemented them.

The World Bank debt buy-back facility

In early 1990 the World Bank set up a limited fund of $100 m. from which IDA-eligible countries can draw to buy back their debt at a significant discount, so that the debtor country can cash in on the secondary-market discount. The amount each country can use at any one time is restricted to $10 m. The facility only addresses the problem of the commercial debt of low-income countries. Furthermore, various restrictions have prevented optimal use being made of the fund. The philosophy behind a multilaterally-backed institution for buying back developing countries' debt and passing on the discounts to the debtor countries is compelling. Just as at an individual-firm level, orderly bankruptcy proceedings, which equitably reduce the claims of the various creditors in order to enable corporate reorganization and a return to activity including borrowing, are acknowledged to be beneficial to both creditors and debtors, so too in the case of sovereign debt, concerted debt reduction is an improvement, both from the point of view of the creditors and of the debtor governments, on the current stalemate where all growth is reduced to a minimum. The rationale for multilateral backing of such a debt-reduction facility or institution is precisely to secure this necessary concertation, and to provide the framework for negotiation rather than unilateral action.

One reason for the exercise of caution before proceeding further in launching determined implementation of such a facility is that the conditions safeguarding against the temptation of unilateral action by certain banks are still not secured. As we have discussed earlier, and as explicitly investigated in the Appendix, the very rumour of an intention to buy back debt tends to cause secondary-market prices to shoot up, in effect almost wiping out the discount. In such circumstances, the utility of the buy-back facility is annihilated. In fact, not only is it the case that many creditor banks are holding out on other conversion mechanisms precisely in the expectation that, sooner or later, such a facility will come up with the effect essentially of bailing them out, but also quite a few speculators have bought debt instruments on the secondary market in the hope of making a capital gain should such a facility be set up.

However, it is possible to conceive of ways of preventing creditors from yielding to this 'free-rider' instinct which in effect annuls the benefits of the mechanism and prevents its being launched. The approach would be one of negotiation among the new multilateral institutions, the debtor countries and the creditors, with the IMF and the World Bank acting as technical advisers and arbiters. One more or less explicit debt-reduction design based on suggestions made by Jeffrey Sachs (op. cit.) involves the following elements[2]:

- the menu of options proposed to creditors (who would not have the choice of opting out except at the risk of finding their claims annulled) would include only alternative ways of achieving significant debt reduction;
- the main instrument for debt reduction would be a lowering of interest rates to sub-market levels on the whole existing stock of debt; alternatively, a large-scale buy-back could be orga- nized through a multilateral facility which would exactly reflect, except for an additional discount, the implicit market value defined by this lower interest rate;
- the IMF and the World Bank would be actively involved in indicating the appropriate level of debt reduction for each individual country;
- these two multilateral institutions would be further entrusted with the responsibility of enforcing adherence to sound macroeconomic policies, with the explicit proviso that non-

[2]See also various proposals and discussions in the Winter 1990 issue of the *Journal of Economic Perspectives*, vol. 4, No 1.

compliance would entail ineligibility for further debt reduction and use of IMF and World Bank resources until the policy stance was corrected;
- regulatory provisos in the creditor countries and other compliance measures would be implemented to ensure equal sharing in the debt-reduction mechanism by all banks and other creditors;
- the design of official lending programmes for each individual debtor country would explicitly take account of the financial implications of debt reduction;
- creditor countries would enact regulatory mechanisms that would support the debt-reduction programme by allowing tax credit for losses and by making the write-down of book values to market values mandatory;
- a policy would be adopted which would explicitly trigger ineligibility for the use of IMF and World Bank resources for countries which accumulated, on a sustained basis, interest arrears *after* a debt-reduction programme had been implemented.

Certain elements of the above scheme are already in place, and there seems to be a desire on the part of certain decision-makers in the multilateral institutions to move towards decisive implementation of some scheme of this type. Already, calls for further diversification of current funding, with bilateral finance beyond the support provided by the World Bank, are receiving encouraging responses. Although limited in its applicability, the IDA buy-back facility, if provided with adequate funding, is capable of significantly alleviating Africa's debt burden, especially when combined with relief on official debt, which constitutes the bulk of low-income African countries' debt.

Brady-style menu-based concerted debt reduction

The Brady Initiative on debt, announced in March 1989, aims at reducing the debt of middle-income countries owed to

commercial banks by using a menu approach, the main elements
of which are:

- securitization, the swapping of old debt for new collateralized
  loans at significant discounts;
- buy-backs of the debt at deep discounts;
- swapping old bank debt for new paper with the same face-
  value but lower interest rates;
- encouragement of the swapping of debt paper for equity shares
  in private or privatized enterprises in the debtor country.

Although the original Brady proposal was vague about the
exact operation of the scheme and on its financial scope, it was
firmly committed to a concerted approach to debt reduction,
calling on commercial banks to waive equal-sharing provisions in
existing loan agreements, and on the multilateral financial
institutions and the donor community to provide financial
support to collateralize a portion of interest payments and debt
obligations, in order to enable use of the securitization item on
the menu. Creditor banks' countries were also urged to adjust
their tax and regulatory regimes, while debtor countries were to
make full use of the plan to reduce their debt while sticking to
their adjustment and economic reform programmes.

Support from the IMF and the World Bank under the plan
provides that up to 25 per cent of extended credits or adjustment
loans can be set aside for debt-reduction operations, either
through buy-backs or the collateralizing of principal. Up to 40
per cent of a country's IMF quota and the equivalent amount
from the World Bank can additionally be provided as interest
support for debt-reduction or debt-service operations. It has been
estimated that, if all countries with recent debt-service difficulties
exercise their maximum rights over the period 1989–92, the plan
would take up an estimated $6 bn of additional IMF resources.
As for the World Bank, maximum use for this purpose will
take up some $2 bn annually. The provisos allow interest-support
funds to be used for debt reduction instead, but do not
allow funds for debt reduction to be used for interest-support
purposes.

During 1990, four concerted debt-reduction agreements were concluded under Brady Plan guidelines. The countries involved were: Mexico, Costa Rica, the Philippines, and Venezuela. Agreement in principle was also reached for Morocco to undertake a debt-reduction operation according to the same plan and with the support of the multilateral financial institutions.

Mexico

Soon after the announcement of the Brady proposals, Mexico made known its debt-reduction plan, which aimed at reducing net debt-service payments from 6 per cent of GDP to 2 per cent. Its initial proposal offered the banks four options:

- to reduce the debt principal by 50 per cent of face-value on $30 bn of loans;
- to reduce the debt interest by an equivalent percentage; this would be accomplished by converting $10 bn of loans into bonds of the same face-value but with interest coupons at 4 per cent;
- to provide new loans equivalent to 80 per cent of interest payments;
- to capitalize 80 per cent of the interest on existing credits.

Under provisions agreed with the IMF and the World Bank, Mexico qualified, at the time, for $1.2 bn for interest support and $2 bn for principal payments or debt buy-back finance. Bilateral support from Japan was also pledged for debt-reduction operations and Mexico was ready to supplement these with its own resources. In June 1989, Mexico obtained World Bank approval for a $1.96 bn loan package, some 25 to 30 per cent of which could be used to back debt reduction by use of collateral. Mexico then proceeded to the final stage of the debt-reduction operation.

In the final agreement the banks had three options:

- to make new loans equivalent to 25 per cent of their current exposure over a four-year period;

- to swap old loans for 30-year bonds paying the same interest as the new loans (i.e. market rates) but with a face-value discounted by 35 per cent (instead of 50 per cent as initially proposed);
- to swap the debt for 30-year bonds paying a 6.25 per cent interest rate (equivalent to a reduction by 4.5 percentage points from the applicable floating rate).

The discounted and fixed-rate bonds carried guarantees of interest for an 18-month servicing, while the principal repayment was guaranteed over 30 years.

Banks representing 49 per cent of the exposure – which amounted to $48.5 bn of medium-and long-term commercial debt, for a *total* debt stock of some $100 bn – chose the third option of the fixed-rate bonds. This part of the deal, while not lowering the nominal debt burden, significantly eased Mexico's interest servicing. The saving was estimated as in the order of $700 m. a year.

The second part of the deal had banks representing 41 per cent of the exposure choose the second option of swapping their debt at a discount of 35 per cent. This transaction reduced a portion of the exposure, equivalent to $20 bn, by some $7 bn. Finally, banks representing 10 per cent of the exposure chose to extend new loans, amounting to $1.2 bn.

Mexico agreed to the provision that the bonds issued under these agreements would not be reschedulable. Furthermore, as usual, the borrowings from the IMF and the World Bank to finance such debt reduction were not reschedulable. These two factors combined to reduce Mexico's future flexibility in its debt management, but the gain was, in addition to the immediate $7 bn debt reduction, an annual saving of $700 m. on interest servicing.

Costa Rica

At end-1989, the government of Costa Rica reached an agreement with its commercial bank creditors to reduce by two-thirds its $1.5 bn debt. The agreement contained a significant amount of debt relief and a capitalization of past interest payments.

In the context of the agreement, the IMF allowed Costa Rica to use 25 per cent of a $50 m. standby loan to buy back its debt on the secondary market.

The final deal involved the banks converting debt according to the following menu:

* a debt buy-back at 16 cents on the dollar;
* debt-service reduction by way of the exchange of old debt for bonds of equal face-value but carrying a lower, fixed interest rate of 6.5 per cent; some of these bonds bore multilateral guarantees from the World Bank and the IMF;
* a separate debt instrument for past due interest claims not retired in the buy-back.

The buy-back covered 60 per cent of Costa-Rica's debt. Money used to pay for the buy-back was borrowed from the World Bank and the IMF and bilaterally from governments. The remaining 40 per cent of the debt was converted by means of two types of bonds. The first, 'enhanced' type, with guarantee, was available to creditors that sold 60 per cent or more of their debt in the buy-back. The bonds carried a 6.25 per cent interest rate with a 30-year repayment period including 10 years' grace. The interest arrears on this portion were refinanced at market rates with a 15-year repayment period. One year of interest on the bonds was guaranteed, while the interest arrears portion carried a rolling guarantee of 3 years of interest. The second type of bond had a coupon interest rate of 6.25 per cent with a 40-year repayment period, including 15 years' grace. They carried no interest-guarantee enhancements. Past due interest carried the same terms as the enhanced bond, but without interest guarantee.

Debt-equity conversion rights were also included in the deal, with $20 m. a year of bonds being exchangeable into local currency investments over a five-year period. One interesting innovation was a value-recovery proviso, whereby the bonds' value would increase if the country achieved certain economic growth targets.

Official support for the programme amounted to $188 m. for the buy-back and $65 m. for interest guarantees. Of the total, $103 m. was provided by the IMF and the World Bank, and the rest through bilateral aid.

The Costa Rican programme has so far been the one Brady-style deal that has yielded significant relief to the debtor, reducing its debt by as much as two-thirds. It could constitute an example for the smaller African countries that have a significant proportion of their external debt owed to commercial bank creditors.

Venezuela

Venezuela reached agreement with its bank creditors in March 1990 on a debt-reduction and debt-restructuring plan covering $21 bn of its commercial debt. The deal offered the following options to the banks:

- provision of new loans equivalent to 20 per cent of the banks' exposure over two years; the new money was to be provided against issues of bonds with a 22-year maturity including 7 years' grace, while the interest rate was at market level;
- the debt could be exchanged for 30-year bonds, with a guarantee of principal and of 14 months' interest; the bonds carried a reduced fixed interest rate of 6.75 per cent, or a floating interest margin of 13/16 points with the face-value written down by 30 per cent;
- a temporary interest-reduction package whereby the banks could swap their old loans for 17-year bonds, with interest of 5 per cent for the first two years, 6 per cent for the next two, 7 per cent for the fifth, and thereafter a floating margin of 7/8 points. Interest collateral was provided for 12 months;
- a cash buy-back at a negotiated price (Venezuelan debt was then selling at 40 cents on the dollar).

The reduction package agreement also included a rescheduling of $19 bn of restructured commercial bank debt, plus another $2.2 bn due to mature in 1994. That portion of the debt was rescheduled over 17 years with a 5-year grace period. Venezuela also successfully resisted calls for a restructuring of the debt of banks not wishing to take any of the above options.

The debt-reduction plan was backed by support from the World Band and the IMF, as well as from bilateral sources.

Over 90 per cent of Venezuela's commercial bank creditors participated in the debt-reduction plan. The outstanding external debt is estimated to be reduced as a result by more than 20 per cent and the annual debt service by about 50 per cent. New money provided is estimated to top $1.15 bn. The scheme covered $21 bn of a total $26.7 bn public sector external debt. The total amount for which the banks chose to exercise options was $18 bn. Of this, over one-third – $6.6 bn – involved option two, the exchange of old debt for 30-year bonds carrying a lowered 6.75 per cent interest and offering zero-coupon US Treasury bonds as guarantee of principal. These bonds also had a fourteen-month guarantee on interest payments. The second largest proportion – slightly less than one-third, or $5.75 bn – involved option one, the exchange of old debt for 17-year bonds with interest at 7/8 per cent over LIBOR and 7 years' grace, but adding new money estimated at $1.15 bn. A proportion amounting to 13.6 per cent of the total $18 bn on which options were exercised involved swapping for new bonds that offered a temporary reduction in interest rate, according to option three above. The amount of debt involved in this item of the menu was $2.44 bn. The remainder was accounted for by the exchange of old debt for new bonds under which the government of Venezuela obtained a 30 per cent reduction in principal ($1.63 bn) and government buy-backs at deep discounts ($1.5 bn).

Philippines

In February 1990, the government of the Philippines agreed with its commercial bank creditors to buy back $1.3 bn of its debt at a discount of 50 cents on the dollar. Financial support for the buy-back came from the IMF, the World Bank, and bilateral donors. During 1990, the IMF released $264 m. to help finance the buy-back, while the World Bank approved a $200 m. loan for use exclusively to buy back the debt.

A month later, the government reached an agreement under which it obtained from its commercial bank creditors a $712 m. new money loan. Together with its regular debt-equity swap operations and other debt-reduction operations, the country had, by April 1990, reduced its $7 bn commercial debt by about $2 bn. In addition, it had, as of that date, a further $850 m. potentially available from the IMF, the World Bank, and bilateral donors, to fund further reduction operations. A swap of old loans for lower-interest bonds was then also being negotiated.

After the severe earthquake in July 1990, the government sought even greater relief, with a 30-month suspension of principal and interest payments. Also, a deferred buy-back programme was proposed to the commercial banks, whereby a new company would be created to repurchase the debt for the Philippines until the country had enough funds to repurchase it, in turn, from the company. A discount of 50 per cent on face-value was envisaged. A debt-for-bonds swap with temporary reductions in interest rates was also sought.

Morocco

Soon after Mexico's zero-coupon-backed debt-reduction deal, Morocco's debt negotiators presented a plan to its bank creditors to reduce a portion amounting to $3.2 bn of the country's $21 bn total debt through a similar zero-coupon-backed swap. By September 1990, the negotiators had signed a two-stage agreement. The first stage would involve pure rescheduling. The banks agreed to reschedule $2.8 bn of debt over 20 years, including 10 years' grace, at an interest rate of LIBOR plus 13/16 per cent; they would also reschedule previously consolidated bankers' acceptances over 15 years including 4 years' grace at the same interest rate. The total amount rescheduled was $7.5 bn.

The second stage was conditional upon Morocco's obtaining an Extended Financing Facility from the IMF before end-December 1991. It involved the banks entering into a debt-reduction agreement offering three options:

* the exchange of old debt for new bonds of equal face-value but with interest rate reduced to the fixed level of 6 5/8 per cent;
* a debt buy-back at a discount to be determined through an auction process; Morocco's debt was then selling at a discount of about 45 per cent;
* the provision of new money amounting to about 13 per cent of the outstanding exposure.

Although the agreement has been secured in principle, the banks have entered into no commitment to participate in the second stage. By mid-year 1991, however, indications were that the second stage would also go through.

Nigeria

By year-end 1990, Nigeria had made proposals to its creditor banks to buy back 60 per cent of its debt, and later included other options much the same as in Costa Rica's deal, reviewed above. The options would be:

* buy-back of 60 per cent of the debt at the discounted price; the secondary-market price was then 32 cents on the dollar;
* conversion of the balance (for banks agreeing to sell at least 60 per cent of their exposure) into 30-year bonds, bearing interest at 6.25 per cent, with a 12-month rolling guarantee of interest; the principal would be secured by 30-year US Treasury zero-coupon bonds;
* the exchange of old debt for new registered bonds carrying interest at LIBOR plus 13/16 per cent, repayable over 20 years including 10 years' grace; banks choosing this option would

in addition provide new loans equivalent to 10 per cent of the amount exchanged.

The agreement in principle covered an amount of $5.8 bn of medium- and long-term debt out of a total debt stock of $32.8 bn, of which $17.5 bn is commercial.

Benefits and drawbacks of menu-based concerted debt reduction

The main advantage of a concerted debt-reduction scheme is that it overcomes problems of collective action. The two most important examples of these are the 'free-rider' problem, and the related secondary-market price effect of voluntary debt-reduction schemes. The 'free-rider' problem arises when some of the creditor banks choose not to participate in debt reduction and hold back on their existing claims. There is strong theoretical and significant empirical evidence to show that a successful debt-reduction deal has the effect of increasing the secondary-market price of the remaining stock of old debt. Thus, if debt-reduction schemes are purely voluntary, the creditors who hold out make a capital gain on their old debt at the expense of those creditors who are ready to participate. There is therefore a disincentive for creditor banks to participate in such schemes even if they perceive them to be in their own interest as well as in the debtor's interest, in line with the 'debt-overhang' argument. By subjecting non-participating banks to a cost for holding out, the concerted approach eliminates the free-rider problem and thereby enhances the efficiency of debt reduction.

The menu-based debt-reduction schemes have taken further advantage of this factor by building into the schemes a process that turns the potential cost to the holding-out creditor into a benefit to the debtor. By requiring creditors who exchanged less than 60 per cent of their debt through the buy-back or lowered-interest options to provide new money, the Costa Rican deal discussed above, for example, turned the possible cost to the holding-out creditor into a benefit to the debtor. Thus the creditor who wants to hold out on 40 per cent or more of his old debt in order to obtain the capital gain of the secondary-market price rise, has to provide new money, with the new debt instrument likely to be discounted back to the new secondary-market price. This discount in the secondary market is immediately appropriated by the debtor.

The problem of the secondary-market price effect has special relevance to the proposal for a multilateral-institution-backed agency to reduce debt. The problem here is that, if participation in debt-reduction schemes remains voluntary rather than concerted, serious negotiations on setting up a new institution are of themselves sufficient to induce creditors to hold on to their loan instruments in order to cash in on the capital gain promised by a rise in secondary-market prices. This disabling effect can be countered only if the debt-reduction process is concerted, with all parties agreeing to the mode and degree of participation and the consequences of their choice in this mode and degree.

It is on these considerations that the greater effectiveness of the menu-based concerted strategy is founded. The menu provides the flexibility, among a set of processes, whereby the creditor can exercise its choice of reduction techniques, depending upon its own assessment of the likely impact on secondary-market prices and on other variables of the debt-reduction transaction. Thus a creditor that has a strong presence in the debtor country may find it most rational to exchange a large proportion of its debt through a debt-equity swap and to provide some new money rather than to sell its debt at a deep discount and/or to lower interest rates. A small bank with limited exposure would prefer a combination of some buy-back and some exchange into lower-interest bonds, or even simply to exit totally through the cash buy-back option. Yet another bank with medium exposure may choose the option of exchange for lower-interest bonds, or make any other choice which it finds rational, given its own expectations.

Thus, the strategy, based both on offering a menu of options and on making the debt-reduction process concerted rather than either voluntary or mandatory, enlarges the choice set both for the creditor and for the debtor, and thereby maximizes the efficiency of the debt-reduction process.

Another important benefit of the menu-based concerted debt-reduction strategy, Brady-style, is that it enables a significant amount of debt relief to be made available to debtor countries where almost none had so far been available from commercial creditors. The figures cited above for the Costa Rican deal illustrate the point very well. About two-thirds of the stock of Costa Rica's debt is likely to be reduced by the deal, and this amount of debt reduction compares favourably with the most ambitious plan proposed for *official* debt relief, namely the (John) Major Plan. It is also very natural and appropriate that the two major African countries that are seriously considering reduction options for their commercial debt should have chosen the Costa Rican deal as their model. These two countries are Nigeria and Morocco.

However, it should be noted in this context that an explicit statement was made by the commercial bank creditors at the time of the Costa Rican deal that the agreement was intended to send the message to sovereign debtors that their best interests would be served by seeking a concerted debt-reduction deal in appropriate time rather than forcing one by accumulating interest arrears. The lesson for African countries with a significant portion of their external debt in commercial form is clear: the Brady-style, menu-based, concerted debt-reduction strategy offers significant potential for commercial bank debt reduction and should be seriously considered. At the same time, credible external debt-management and macroeconomic policies must be pursued and early approaches made to commercial creditors in order to put in place an efficient debt-reduction programme. As was the case with IMF-backed austerity programmes a decade back, delaying until the problem gets out of hand before envisaging hard solutions only complicates the issue.

At the same time, however, it must be recognized that the Brady-style strategy has one serious shortcoming that could possibly be considered fatal for African countries. Its potential for mobilizing new money is extremely limited, despite the innovative approaches in tailoring programmes to achieve that end. Yet enhanced access to international capital inflows to meet their development needs is absolutely crucial to African countries. What is worse, even successful debt reduction through the operations investigated above has not enhanced the creditworthiness of most Latin American countries to the point of making new commercial bank credit available to any significant degree. It remains to be seen whether foreign-investor confidence will recover strongly enough to make a difference in that source of foreign capital.

The situation for African countries is much bleaker. While significant relief of the *official* debt of the low-income countries of Africa would provide a part solution to the continent's debt and growth problems, it seems clear that, beyond the positive effects of the Brady Plan and innovative approaches taken in that context, more needs to be done for African countries. Two possibilities suggest themselves. The first is upgrading of the Brady Initiative to increase the effectiveness of its new-money thrust, with special mechanisms built in to address the particular problems of African low-and middle-income countries with a significant proportion of their external debt in commercial form. The second is the total transformation of the IDA debt buy-back facility into a new International Debt Facility that addresses the commercial debt not only of low-income, but also of lower-middle-income, countries. The new institution's resources should be increased several-fold from its present puny $100 m. and its articles should contain special provisions to encourage new capital inflows into African countries.

Recommendations

The study of the various types of market-based debt-reduction schemes that have so far been utilized by the middle-income indebted countries with a significant proportion of commercial debt yields lessons from which pertinent recommendations can be derived for African countries facing similar situations. We derive our recommendations by asking five questions about full-fledged debt-equity conversion programmes, ad hoc debt-equity conversion, debt buy-backs, menu-based debt reduction, and collective action by African countries.

A. Should any given African country have a full-fledged debt-equity conversion programme?

A.1. *Preconditions for success*

This study has highlighted the preconditions necessary for the success of a full-fledged debt-equity conversion programme. Firstly, pronounced disequilibria should have been eliminated from the general macroeconomic relationships such as the balance of payments, price-level movements, budgetary performance, money-supply movements and domestic debt management including deficit financing. Disequilibria in these relationships distort the market signals – prices, wages, interest rates – sent to economic operators, and induce additional unnecessary riskiness and uncertainty that may turn the envisaged benefits of a debt-equity programme into costs, *ex post*. Secondly, the retrenchment of government intervention in the economy should have proceeded far enough, otherwise would-be investors will feel that the scope for profitable activity is too narrow, and they may fear unfair competition from government-subsidized enterprises. Thirdly, credit allocation, exchange-rate stabilization and foreign trade policies should have become sufficiently liberalized not to penalize the domestic investor vis-à-vis his foreign counterpart who, in addition to the incentives he gets from investment through debt-equity conversion, may have access to easier credit from abroad and may not have to bear an excess burden in obtaining foreign exchange.

A.2. *Which African countries would benefit from a full-fledged debt-equity conversion programme?*

The study has stressed that the scope for African countries significantly to reduce their debt stock and debt service through the debt-equity conversion mechanism is rather limited. But there are other benefits from debt-equity conversion programmes like the encouragement of foreign investment, incentives to repatriate flight capital, technology transfer and so forth. Therefore, even countries that may not qualify for full-fledged debt-equity programmes may benefit from carrying out ad hoc debt-equity conversions.

Countries likely to benefit from full-fledged programmes should have relatively diversified economies, their debt must be selling at a significant discount, and they must have an investment code that is attractive to foreign investors, as well as meeting the preconditions specified above. The following countries were identified in the text as likely to benefit from full-fledged debt-equity conversion programmes: Côte d'Ivoire, Egypt, Ghana, Kenya, Morocco, Nigeria, Tunisia, Zaire.

A.3. *What are the modalities of programme implementation?*

For the countries that *do* put such programmes in place, the more suitable pricing and allocation mechanism is the auction system, as opposed to administrative pricing. The secondary-market price can be used as a good indicator, but not dogmatically as a baseline reference.

The following technical and legal requirements relating to the micro-management of the debt, and institutional set-ups relating to debt-equity conversion proper, are among the administrative pre-requisites for a successful programme.

Technical issues

i. proper documentation must be in place regarding the original contracts and terms;
ii. there must be a precise breakdown of the debt totals according to creditors;
iii. there must be a similar breakdown of debt totals according to borrowers and/or purposes where parastatal bodies have contracted publicly guaranteed debt, or where private external debt exists;
iv. competent information processing of secondary-market prices and developments on the market must be put in place.

Legal requirements

i. necessary permission must be sought from creditors during rescheduling to waive 'equal treatment' clauses;

ii. creditor-country regulatory and tax measures must be studied and followed in order to tailor incentives accordingly.

Institutional requirements

i. the setting-up of an investment-screening unit is required to determine which projects are on the priority lists, so as to maximize the benefits from debt conversion;

ii. there is a need to set up a monitoring unit to track the use of the local-currency proceeds of debt conversion, and for administering blocked accounts;

iii. it is necessary to build up added analytical capacity to assess the economy-wide impact of debt conversion via the monetary and fiscal processes;

iv. the choice of the auction mechanism and the determination of commissions to the implementing agency have to be decided.

Four supplementary recommendations are in order regarding the administrative process. They emerge from the experience of countries currently implementing full-fledged programmes.

i. the administrative safeguard of using blocked accounts into which the conversion proceeds go initially should be put in place to prevent abuse;

ii. no interest should be paid on the blocked accounts;

iii. undue encumbering of the approval process, apart from taking the above-mentioned safeguards, should be avoided;

iv. the primary focus of debt-equity conversion should be on debt reduction, and added incentives to attract foreign investment should be provided outside the scope of the programme. In particular, the provision of an exchange-rate subsidy is inadvisable.

A.4. *Likely problems and solutions*

Two major problems are likely: inflation and round-tripping. To tackle the inflation problem, the only effective solution that has emerged is that of putting a ceiling on the quantity of conversion allowed for given periods. The ceilings should be in line with monetary policies and credit targets. Dovetailing debt-equity conversion with privatization also helps, because government credit requirements decrease in parallel with the additional injection of liquidity caused by conversion, and overall credit expansion is thus kept under control. As for round-tripping, the use of blocked accounts for the initial payment of the conversion proceeds, coupled with sourcing requirements for the foreign exchange with which the debt instrument is bought in the first place, usually suffice to tackle the round-tripping problem.

B. For those countries envisaging only ad hoc debt-equity conversion transactions, what should be the appropriate strategy?

It has been argued in this study that, while relatively few African countries are likely to benefit significantly, on a net basis, from full-fledged debt-equity conversion programmes, most are likely to derive some gain from ad hoc transactions. Two important recommendations in this context are that, first, it is *not* necessary to use intermediary services or to impose their use, with attendant costs, on potential investors, and, secondly, it is inadvisable to provide an exchange-rate subsidy in the debt-conversion transaction. It is desirable and possible to keep track of the use of conversion proceeds without getting entrapped in costly administrative machinery, and the problems both of inflation and of round-tripping diminish.

C. Which countries are likely to benefit most from debt buy-backs?

The scope for debt buy-back is quite significant for economically stronger countries that can generate some excess reserves with which to finance a buy-back. African countries that envisage this method of debt reduction can expect a discount of 50 per cent as a minimum and can often do better. The important consideration in deciding on a buy-back is the opportunity cost of the alternative use of reserves. However, recent initiatives by the multilateral financial institutions provide for the use of part of the borrowed resources for debt-reduction operations, and the opportunity of using this window to bring about debt reduction deserves careful consideration.

D. Which approach is most suitable for Brady-style, menu-based debt-reduction schemes?

This study has found many attractive features in Brady-style, menu-based debt-reduction schemes, not the least of which is the possibility they open for concerted debt reduction, where so far commercial creditors have insisted on voluntary approaches. Only two African countries (Nigeria and Morocco) have so far secured agreement in principle to conduct such debt-reduction programmes. One of the more successful such programmes – the Costa Rican example – provided debt reduction of about 66 per cent to the debtor country, a level equivalent to that of one of the most liberal *official* debt-relief proposals, the John Major plan.

Therefore a menu-based debt-reduction programme tailored on the Costa Rican model is strongly recommended for the low-income African countries that have a significant proportion of their debt owed to commercial creditors, as well as for lower-middle-income African countries. The programme should offer at least four options: buy-backs at significant discounts, exchange for lower-interest bonds, provision of new money equivalent to a certain percentage of exposure for creditors not exchanging a sufficiently high proportion of their debt, and exchange of bonds for lower face-value but securitized new bonds. In the context of the agreement for such debt-reduction deals, countries might also negotiate separate debt-equity swap possibilities, depending on each country's aptitude as spelt out above.

E. What should African countries do collectively?

This study has argued that, while Brady-style menu-based debt-reduction schemes provide significant potential for tackling African countries' debt problems, they do not adequately meet present expectations. The most promising avenue for African countries collectively to exercise their influence to obtain more leverage in debt reduction is to negotiate an enlargement of the present IDA debt buy-back facility, first to increase its resources considerably, secondly to allow menu-based debt-reduction operations, and thirdly to include lower-middle-income countries. It is conceivably possible even to push for the earmarking of a certain percentage of the resources of such an enlarged International Debt Facility to tackle African countries' commercial debt problems. Coupled with initiatives recommended in the related study on official debt relief, such collective action could open up avenues for effective reduction of Africa's external debt burden.

Appendix

Secondary-Market Pricing and Various Types of Conversion

Consider a country that has an external debt of US$10 bn, and an uncertain foreign-exchange income flow (a situation typical of most, if not all, indebted developing countries), which we characterize here, for simplicity,[1] by a uniform probability density function defined over the interval (0 to 1.0). The initial

---

[1]Clearly, other methods of analysing debt-conversion exercises, including valuation of debt under uncertainty of foreign-exchange income flow by the debtor, are possible. The most general approach is contained in Elhanan Helpman's two studies: *The Simple Analytics of Debt Equity Swaps and Debt Forgiveness*, IMF Working Paper 88/30 (1988) and *Voluntary Debt Reduction: Incentives and Welfare*, IMF Working Paper WP 88/84 (September 1988).

secondary-market price of debt, assuming market participants accept the uniform probability function just mentioned as their common *a priori* subjective probability distribution function, would be 50 cents to the dollar, or US$5 bn for the total debt. This figure derives from the mean of the distribution function. But the subjective probability distribution from the debtor's point of view needs not be the same as that of the market participants: in fact, the typical debtor country follows an economic strategy that it hopes will increase its foreign-exchange income stream, and therefore typically has a more optimistic subjective probability distribution. Again for simplicity, let us assume this is uniform but now defined over the interval (0.1 to 1.1). The valuation of the debt, from the debtor's point of view, is 55 cents to the dollar or US$5.5 bn for the total debt, again reflecting the mean of this other probability distribution function. Two compelling reasons argue for the assumption of a more optimistic subjective probability function from the debtor's perspective: first, the one just mentioned about efforts to increase external revenues; second, the fact that, at this stage, the debtor is still committed to pay the full contractual value of the debt in order to ensure continued future access to international capital markets, and although repudiation and/or forcing a relief operation is a real option, it is not accounted for in the formulation of the subjective probability distribution because that represents the dominant strategy, *at this point*. Furthermore, it should be noted that, *for the time being*, the creditors' and independent market participants' subjective probability distribution is the same, but it needs not be so at other times, as we shall see.

The market discount on the debt from the creditors' point of view is 50 per cent, while it is 45 per cent from the debtor's point of view. This five-percentage-point margin defines an area of Pareto sub-optimal states which can be exploited to mutual advantage by moving towards Pareto optimality. The debtor, however, cannot exploit this opportunity, because his cost of borrowing presumably carries a risk-premium higher than the five percentage points, and he has no resources not committed to alternative uses which would not yield a better return. The opportunity does not constitute an attractive transaction for the creditor, because he feels the real discount factor is 50 per cent.

Suppose, now, the debtor country benefits from a windfall foreign-exchange inflow of $1 bn. Its *a priori* subjective probability distribution is fulfilled *a posteriori*. This triggers a number of reactions from all economic units, including debtor, creditor and independent market participants, if a secondary market for debt instruments exists. If alternative uses for the windfall funds are less attractive, the debtor can buy back part of his debt on the secondary market and benefit from the discount. Other market participants also wish to purchase the debt instruments because now the probability distribution of repayments has shifted favourably. But even if they do not buy any portion of the debt instruments outstanding, a revaluation of the debt on the secondary market occurs. Lastly, the creditors could act like independent market participants themselves and buy back part or all of the debt offered for sale, in effect withdrawing it from the market and revaluing it upwards.

What is the new equilibrium price of debt, and who benefits from the various possible deals, and to what extent? The answer to this question depends on:[2]

i. the shape of the subjective probability distribution of future foreign-exchange earnings, which is here assumed to be uniform. We shall concentrate exclusively on this easier case.

ii. the type of debt conversion envisaged. It is important here to note that the valuation of the debt and the distribution of benefits will be different according to whether the conversion is a buy-back (self-financed or third-party-financed), a collateralization (by way of interest guaranteeing, principal guaranteeing, interest and principal guaranteeing or commodity indexing) arrangement, or a debt-equity swap. The valuation of debt and the distribution of benefits will also depend on what portion of the outstanding debt total is being converted (we focus only on the more realistic case of *partial* rather than total conversion).

iii. the assumptions behind the characterization of the market

---

[2]It must be noted that, once the secondary-market price is established after all market participants have reacted competitively to the conversion announcement, then *all* conversion schemes yield the *same* amount of debt reduction.

and the reactions of market participants. Here, we assume perfectly competitive behaviour, with full and costless information, such as is commonplace in ordinary economic analysis. Hence, strategic analysis is ruled out.

To turn back, then, to our example of a country with a total external debt of $10 bn, with an uncertain foreign-exchange income flow characterized by a subjective probability distribution of uniform shape defined over the interval (0 to 1.0). The windfall gain of $1 bn could be used by the debtor country to buy back its debt on the secondary market; this is a self-financed buy-back. Alternatively, and more generally from an analytical point of view, one can analyse a third-party-financed buy-back where one assumes that a market participant offers to buy part – here one-tenth, being $1 bn out of a total of $10 bn – of the total outstanding debt in a single auction, and promises to forgive the difference between the auction price, PA, at which he purchases the bonds, and the contractual value of the bonds purchased. Working with value *per dollar*, it turns out that the amount forgiven per dollar of total debt would be $1/10 (1 - PA)$. Now, the way the conversion system is assumed to operate is that the market participant buys the defined proportion of the debt, and then issues new contracts with face-value per dollar equal to the market price after the auction. But under full information and perfect competition, the creditors revise their *a priori* subjective probability distribution, and revalue their market price for the new contract to the post-auction market price PM.

How, then, does market equilibrium determine the value of PM? First, it should be remembered that the market price is the expected value of an uncertain flow of payments characterized by a uniform probability distribution. There are two distinct sets of outcomes to be distinguished: those where foreign-exchange inflows are equal to or greater than PA, that is, when the probability that new contracts will be fully paid off is unity, and those where foreign-exchange inflows are less than PA. Since the market PM is computed *per dollar*, we then have:

$$PM = 1/2 \; (1 - 1/10(1 - PA)) + 1/10 \; (1 - PA).$$

The first term in the right-hand side of the above equation is of the form indicated because the probability distribution is uniform: it indicates the expected value of payment per dollar for the two sets of outcomes.

Next, in equilibrium, we must have PM = PA, that is, the post-auction market price must equal the auction 1 price because otherwise arbitrage opportunities would continue to exist and the market price continue to adjust. Therefore, market equilibrium determines the post-auction market price as:

$$PM = 1/2 \ (1 - 1/10(1 - PA)) + 1/10 \ (1 - PM)$$

Therefore PM = $PA/21 = 52.4 cents to the dollar.

The above analysis explains how, by using this secondary-market mechanism for a debt-forgiveness operation, a market participant can impart to the aid-dollar earmarked for debt forgiveness considerable additional mileage, by capitalizing on the Pareto-improving opportunities offered by differing and adjustable *a priori* subjective probability distributions of repayments prospects. The same analysis can be used to study a straight buy-back by the debtor country itself, out of proceeds of windfall foreign-exchange earnings and without third-party-financed forgiveness, and the results would show similar additional mileage given to the buy-back dollar, thanks to secondary-market-assisted debt conversion. For the time being, we concentrate on the third-party-financed forgiveness case, to decide the net result of the buy-back-with-forgiveness operation into its component parts.

The debt-conversion exercise results in three distinguishable effects. First, the market discount is reduced from 50 per cent to 47.6 per cent, since from a secondary-market price of 50 cents to the dollar, the price of debt has increased to 52.4 cents. This increased creditworthiness of the debtor country reflects the improved prospects of its meeting its debt obligations after a portion of its debt has been cancelled through buy-back. What is more, this improved creditworthiness would result is an 'investment benefit' to the debtor country equal to the present value of all future investments[3] undertaken at this new discount

---

[3]By 'investments', we mean additional loans as well as direct and/or portfolio investments.

rate which would not have been undertaken at the initial 50 per cent discount. The precise calculation of this benefit would require knowledge of the empirical investment curve in the debtor country, but despite its immediately unquantifiable nature, this benefit constitutes the main advantage of a debt-conversion exercise for lower- or upper-middle-income countries with relatively good growth potential but a serious current and foreseeable shortage of capital.

The second effect relates to the immediate capital gain of the debtor country. This is measured by the amount of debt forgiven, multiplied by the probability of outcomes where foreign-exchange income flows exceed (1 − (amount forgiven). The amount of debt forgiven per dollar of total debt is $1/10(1 = PM) = $1/10 (1 − 11/21) = $1/21. The probability that foreign-exchange income flows exceed (1 − (amount forgiven) is given by $1/2\{1/10(1 − 11/21)\} = 1/42$. Therefore the immediate capital gain works out to $1/882 per dollar of debt outstanding, or $11.34 m. for a total debt outstanding of $10 bn, with $1 bn bought back. This works out to only 1.1 per cent pure capital gain.

Third, the creditors realize a capital gain equal to $240 m. since the market value of their debt holdings increases from $5 bn to $5.24 bn as a result of the forgiveness operation. Now, the capital gain of $240 m. accrues to the initial creditors regardless of their participation in the auction or not. It may be possible to increase the debtor country's capital gain and give some more incentives to participants in the forgiveness scheme, by subordinating the debt of initial creditors who do not participate in the scheme to those who do. If this additional proviso is added to the scheme, an amount of $216 m. (= 9/10 of $240 m.) would be released from non-participating creditors' gains. The end-result would be a substantial hike in the debtor country's immediate capital gain to something much more substantial than the 1.1 per cent under a scheme without subordination provisos. Concomitantly, however, the 'investment benefit' may be reduced, since the subordination of old debt would adversely affect the psychology of potential investors.

Index